REVD KENNETH ALFRED ALMOND, the eldest son of a blacksmith's striker (labourer), was born in St Helens, Lancashire, in 1936. Leaving school at fifteen, he worked for twenty-three years in a number of clerical positions in St Helens, a then-thriving glass-industry and coal mining town, and also Liverpool. He worked for the Church Missionary Society in the Dioceses of Lincoln, Ely and Peterborough for five years and was ordained to the diaconate of the Church of England in Boston, Lincolnshire, in 1979. He then entered the priesthood in Lincoln Cathedral the following year. He served in the Lincoln Diocese as a parish priest and rural dean for twenty years, but since retirement has devoted his time to writing and the study of south-west Lancashire history.

FRONT COVER IMAGE: This stained-glass window can be seen at the rebuilt Roman Catholic Church of St Anne and Blessed Dominic, Sutton, St Helens, Merseyside. It depicts five of the Forty Martyrs: John Almond (top centre in chasuble); John Rigby (top left); Margaret Clitherow (top right); John Wall (centre left); Edmond Arrowsmith (centre right); Thomas More (bottom left) and John Fisher (bottom right).

Saint John Almond and the Society of his Time

Saint John Almond and the Society of his Time

Revd Kenneth Alfred Almond

Best wishes
Ken.

ATHENA PRESS
LONDON

SAINT JOHN ALMOND AND THE SOCIETY OF HIS TIME
Copyright © Revd Kenneth Alfred Almond 2008

All Rights Reserved

No part of this book may be reproduced in any form
by photocopying or by any electronic or mechanical means,
including information storage or retrieval systems,
without permission in writing from both the copyright
owner and the publisher of this book.

ISBN: 978 1 84748 366 9

First published 2008 by
ATHENA PRESS
Queen's House, 2 Holly Road
Twickenham TW1 4EG
United Kingdom

Every effort has been made to trace the copyright holders of
works quoted within this book and obtain permissions.
The publisher apologises for any omission and will be happy to
make necessary changes in subsequent print runs.

Printed for Athena Press

*To my wife, Hilary,
and my sons Martin and Richard,
with love and thanks for everything.*

History with its flickering lamp stumbles along the trail of the past, trying to reconstruct its scenes, to revive its echoes, and kindle with pale gleams the passion of former days.

Sir Winston Spencer Churchill,
12 November 1940, House of Commons

The recorded past is available for us to discover. We can define our personal heritage at almost any time it is convenient for us to do so. The recent past and the present are not easy to discover.

Unknown

Contents

Foreword — 11

The Almond Connection? — 12

John Almond's Birth and Early Life, 1576–1597 — 13

- A Question of Genealogy — 13
- John's Schooling at Woolton — 19
- John's Stay in Ireland — 20
- John Almond's Parish Church — 21
- The Parish of Childwall — 26
- The Parish of Prescot — 28

Catholics in South-west Lancashire — 31

Lord Burghley's Map of Lancashire — 33

John Almond's World — 35

- The Secret Chapels of South West Lancashire — 35
- The River Mersey – Birkenhead to Liverpool Ferry — 42

Contemporary People and Events in and Around the Time of John Almond — 43

- St Margaret Clitherow of York, 1556–1586 — 43
- Robert Middleton, 1570–1601 — 44

William Shakespeare, 1564–1616	45
Guy Fawkes, 1570–1606	47
John Donne, 1572–1631	48
The Armada – 1588	49
British Hanging	49
Queen Elizabeth I, 1533–1603	51
The Venerable English College, Rome	57
King James I of England	63
John Almond's Later Life	66
The Missionary Priest, 1602–1612	66
First Arrest – 1607	68
Time in Jail	74
The Trial	77
The Martyrdom of John Almond	80
The World Shortly after John Almond's Martyrdom	85
The Pilgrim Fathers – 1620	85
The Forty Martyrs of England and Wales	88
Bibliography	91

 # Foreword

As I am an Anglican (Church of England) priest with the surname Almond – the only one recorded in *Crockford's Clerical Directory* for some years – I found an entry for Saint John Almond, a Catholic missionary priest, in *The Oxford Dictionary of Saints* by David Hugh Farmer, most interesting:

> ALMOND, John (c.1577–1612), priest and martyr. Born at Allerton (Lancs), he was educated mainly in Ireland until he became a student at the English College, Rome, in 1597. In 1601 he was ordained priest and obtained his doctorate in divinity, after showing himself exceptionally intelligent and quick in disputation. In 1602 he returned to England, where for seven years he was an energetic and successful itinerant missionary. Pursuivants captured him and he was imprisoned, first at Newgate, then at the Gatehouse. Either he escaped or he was released, for there is a record of him working in Staffordshire in 1609, but in 1612 he was again arrested and imprisoned in the appalling conditions of Newgate. Because of his high reputation for holiness and learning, the Archbishop of Canterbury and other divines tried to extract a recantation from him, but without success. In 1612 he was accused and convicted of being a priest, although the charge was never proved, and he was executed at Tyburn on 5 December. He was canonised by Paul VI, in 1970 as one of the Forty Martyrs of England and Wales. Feast: 25 October.[1]

According to the Childwall Parish Church registers, John Amott (Almond) seems to have had brothers and sisters.

I have carried out extensive research, quarried and visited assiduously and assembled a vast amount of material, all of which now comes together in this text.

---

[1] From: Farmer, D H (ed.), *The Oxford Dictionary of Saints*, Oxford University Press, 1978. By permission of Oxford University Press.

The Almond Connection?

I was born in St Helens, Lancashire, which is approximately seven miles from Allerton (now a south-eastern suburb of Liverpool) – the birthplace of John Almond.

I may have a genealogical connection with John, even if only collaterally. There are many Almond families in south-west Lancashire; professional researchers imply that the first record of the name Almond is in the counties of Yorkshire and Northumberland.

My research of the 'Almond connection' has brought me to around 1710, approximately 134 years short of John's birth in Allerton. It is interesting, however, that Christian names used in John's family are used in my ancestors over this 300-year period: William, Ellin, James, Richard, John, Henry, Thomas and Anne.

Most of my Almond ancestors lived in the Lancashire area: Moss Bank, Windle (now part of St Helens), Billinge and Upholland.

As a schoolboy in St Helens, we were taught that our town had the second largest percentage of Catholic population in England – the largest being in Preston, Lancashire. The 1881 census shows many Irish families living in St Helens' slums after the 1849–1852 Irish potato famine. This would certainly have had a bearing on the Catholic population of 33%. Irish immigrants numbering 1,241,410 arrived in the city of Liverpool, and then dispersed to locations around the world, including St Helens.

 # John Almond's Birth and Early Life, 1576–1597

A QUESTION OF GENEALOGY

John Almond, alias Lathom, alias Molyneux (two local family names) was born at Allerton, now a south-eastern suburb of Liverpool, approximately two miles from Childwall parish church, and he was almost certainly born of Catholic parents. The great family of Lathom who had owned Allerton Hall from Norman times and Lord Molyneux of Croxteth Hall were both staunch Catholics, and they would have had a great influence on John and his family. In the sixteenth century Woolton, Speke and Allerton are referred to as hamlets. It is recorded in *Memoirs of Missionary Priests* (finished in 1741–1742) that John Almond was born on the 'skirts of Allerton'[2]. In *Liverpool's Hidden Story* it is recorded that he was born in Lancashire on the 'borders of Allerton and Speke'[3]. Allerton is approximately two miles from Speke Hall, a large timber-framed manor house built in the medieval and Tudor period. When questioned in 1612 by John King, Bishop of London (1611–1621) as to where he was born, John answered, 'About Allerton – I was not born in Allerton, but in the edge or side of Allerton'[4]. On the gallows waiting to be hanged, he confessed that he was born in Lancashire, that the town's name was South Allerton and this was where he was brought up until he was about eight years old.

---

[2] From: Challoner, Bishop Richard, *Memoirs of Missionary Priests,* London, Burns Oates & Westbourne, 1924, p.329
[3] From: Stonor, Robert Julian, *Liverpool's Hidden Story*, UK, Birchley Hall Press, 1957, p.39
[4] From: Challoner, *Memoirs of Missionary Priests,* p.330

John's christening at All Saints Parish Church in Childwall is recorded as happening on 20 January 1576. The dating would actually be 1576–1577 as, at that time, 25 March was New Year's Day; the Julian calendar devised by Julius Caesar still being in use at that time. The original entry – written on parchment bound in a leather register – reads John Amott (Almond). The register

> ...was made in the yeare of our Lord 1598 and contayning such Weddings Christenings & Buryals as have bin there Registered from the yere of our Lord 1557.[5]

It was probably originally recorded on loose-leaf pages. His father's name is not given. However, a marriage is recorded between Thomas Amonde and Alice Orme on 1 July 1565, as well as a marriage between Richard Amott and an unknown woman on 5 May 1559 – could one of these couples be his parents? In the second recusant roll (1593–1594), there is an entry of 'Alice Almond – lately of Allerton in the foresaid parish, widow'[6]. The vicar at the time of the baptism was David Calton. The register records:

> [1588] This yere dyed Sir David Catton (or Calton) vicar of Childwall. And after him came to serve in his place Mr Edmond Hoppwood: vide buryalls.[7]

A search among the list of wills at Chester gives us, in many cases, several generations of the same family resident in the township. Thus during the sixteenth, seventeenth and eighteenth centuries there are names of numerous members of the Almond (or Amott) family (also of Woolton).

There are also the baptisms recorded; maybe brothers, sisters or cousins of John:

---

[5] From: LPRS, *Registers of the Parish of Childwall – Part I 1577–1680*, Lancashire Parish Register Society, volume 106
[6] From: Bowler, Dom Hugh (ed.), *Recusant Rolls No 2 1593–1594*, London, Catholic Truth Society, 1965, p.84
[7] Ibid.

John Almond's Birth and Early Life, 1576–1597

1560	5 December	William Amott
1563	8 June	Ales Amott
1566	23 February	Ellin Amott
1567	5 December	James Amott
1569	11 November	William Amott
1572	22 February	Jane Amott
1576	13 August	Richard Amott
	17 October	Jane Amott
1576/7	**20 January**	**John Amott**
1577	2 March	Elizabeth Amott
1578	23 January	John Amott
1579	4 December	Henry Amott
1580	31 January	Henry Amott
	11 April	Henry Amott
1581	30 May	Thomas Amott
1582	7 April	Henry Amott
1582	30 May	Alice Amott
1583	2 March	Elizabeth Amott
1584	15 August	Ales Amott
	28 December	Thomas Amott
1585	29 August	Anne Amott

In *The Seminary Priests Volume 1* Anstruther says that John had a brother called Henry – it could possibly be the same Henry baptised on 4 December 1579, 31 January 1580, 11 April 1580 or 7 April 1582. Another Henry also died on 11 April 1580. In the year of John's martyrdom, there is a baptism on 18 May 1612 of Johannes, son of Henrici Almond. Could this be John's nephew, named after him? John did sign himself as Ioannes Almondus in the English College, Rome.

There are also the marriages recorded around this time:

1559	5 May	Richard Amott
1565	1 July	Thomas Amonde and Alice Orme
1583	21 August	Thomas Amott and Elizabeth Plombe

Saint John Almond and the Society of his Time

1586	16 April	William Ireland and Alice Amott
1591	3 July	William Amott and Margarett Cock
1596	22 August	Thomas Whyte and Anna Almond
1605	28 June	Thomas Alcar and Letticia Almott
1607	30 April	Thomas Almond and Margaret Burrowes
1608	22 May	Henricus Almond and Dorothea Vose

These are the burials recorded[8]:

1558	12 February	Henry Amott
1559	5 May	Richard Amott
1564	26 July	Henry Amott
1571	8 September	John Amott
1578	8 April	Margery Amott
1580	11 April	Henry Amott
1582	15 May	Rychard Amott
1582	30 May	Alice Amott
1588	28 April	ux. Alexander Amott
1588	20 May	Alexander Amott
1595	21 June	fa. Jacobi Amott
1597	16 May	fa. Alexandri Amott
1608	9 March	Eliz: Almond sp.
1609	20 April	Thomas Almond
1612	7 October	Alicia ux. Henrici Almond

An act was passed in 1751, nearly two-hundred years after John's baptism, for the change of the style of the calendar. Many protested; some firmly. The act provided that the legal year in

---

[8] ux. – *uxor* – wife; fa – *filia* – daughter; fs – *filius* – son

John Almond's Birth and Early Life, 1576–1597

England in 1752 should commence on 1 January instead of 25 March. It further laid down that after 3 September of that year the next ensuing day should be called the 14th. Thus eleven days were dropped out of the calendar of 1752. The loss of the eleven days caused an outcry. Some firmly believed that it meant cutting eleven days from their lives. Regulations were introduced concerning the days for fairs and markets and new tables were created for the moveable feasts. In adopting the new style, England was two centuries behind the rest of Europe, except Russia. The change was well received by Catholic countries because it was Pope Gregory XIII who decreed the change in his bull of 1582. For centuries it has been recognised that the Julian calendar made the year eleven minutes and fourteen seconds too long. By the time of Pope Gregory, it had fallen back ten days, having fallen back at a rate of three days every four-hundred years. To prevent the discrepancy occurring again, the bull introduced a revision in the leap years. For a long time there was much confusion in England in the attempts to reconcile the dates in England with those on the continent and in Scotland. Scotland adopted the change in 1600 and made 1 January the beginning of their year. Therefore, the Elizabethan New Year of 1577, when John was born, began on the Annunciation of the Blessed Virgin Mary – 25 March – known as Lady Day, in honour of the Feast of the Annunciation.

The majority of English people are unlikely to be able to trace a continuous line of family beyond the sixteenth century when Elizabeth made parish registers compulsory. The most important source of genealogical information prior to the beginning of civil registration in 1837 and the first census returns of 1841 are undoubtedly the parish registers. The system of parish registration of baptisms, marriages and burials officially began in 1538. In 1597 it was ordered that a special register should be kept, and previous loose-sheet records should be entered in the book. The minister and churchwardens were charged with signing each page as a true transcript thus: 'A note of a Constitution for keeping of Register books in Churches agreed upon the 25 October 1597 Eliz: 39'[9].

---

[9] From: *Childwall Registers*, 1557–1680, volume 106, p.186

Saint John Almond and the Society of his Time

> Everie Church shall have a booke of parchment that the names of all Christened, maryed and buryed maybe therein Registered.
>
> That the names of all suche as have bine christened, maryed and buryed within your parish and since the beginning of her ma[jes]ties raigne shalbe wrytten into the new parchment booke.
>
> Uppon everye Sondaye the parson, vicar or curate after morning or evening prayer shall reade openlie what was registered everye day that weeke and att thend of everye leaffe, the Minister and Churchwardens shall subscribe their names, which beinge done, they shall locke up safelye the said booke in a chest provyded for that purpose with three keyes, whereof one shalbe with the minister, thother two with the Churchwardens, that the sayde booke shall neither be taken forth of the chest, neither putt into the chest without the presence of the minister and churchwardens. 1598
>
> Edmond Hopwood (or Edmund Hapwood) – Vicar
John Pasmage – churchwarden
John Whitfield – churchwarden
Robert Quick schoolem[aste]r and wryter hereof[10]

Some years ago, I was fortunate enough to see a valuable set of records of births, marriages and burials covering almost the entire period from 1557 to the end of the eighteenth century for the parish of Childwall. They are detailed thus in the church terrier[11] for 1778:

1. 1557–1612 (sound and entire)
2. 1653–1703 (much torn and imperfect)
3. 1703–1753 (very clean and correct)
4. 1753 (in use)
5. 1754–1772 (marriages only)
6. 1772 (in use: marriages only)[12]

---

[10] Ibid.
[11] A church terrier is a statement of the assets belonging to the church at any specific time; the terriers include land, property, income from tithes, vestments, the communion plate, registers and any ornaments of value belonging to the church. It is still legally binding for each parish church to keep an up-to-date terrier.
[12] From the church terrier at All Saints Parish Church, Childwall, Liverpool.

Since then some of the missing records have been found, accounting for the years 1625–1638. They were in a very bad condition but were repaired as far as possible and placed with the other records in 1912, having been missing for at least 130 years.

By the early sixteenth century, the population of England was once again beginning to increase as the incidence of the bubonic plague of 1349 declined.

The Elizabethan law determined that Catholics, if they were to keep out of prison or preserve themselves from fines, had to have their babies baptised in the Protestant Church before they were a month old. They could not have their children baptised legally by the Catholic rite by a Catholic priest. It has been commonly stated that baptisms took place three days after birth. It is therefore possible that John was born on 17 January 1576/7.

There were many variations of the surname Almond – Amott, Allmond, Almott, Aumond, Allmond, Allman, Amonde, Almand, Allamand and Awmond. John was recorded at his baptism as Amott and at Rome in Latin as Ioannes Almondus. In *Romance of Names (1914)*, it is suggested that the name Almond was given to someone coming from a distance:

> ...Allman (Allemand), often perverted to Almond, were considered a sufficient mark of identification for men who came from foreign parts.[13]

Allemand is French for 'German'. This would not mean that they were French or German, just that they were from a foreign clime. He suggests that Almond was so common a name in the Middle Ages it must have occasionally descended from the Anglo-Saxon word meaning 'descendant of Aethelmund'. Variations of spelling frequently occurred, even between father and son.

JOHN'S SCHOOLING AT WOOLTON

There is a traditional belief that John Almond went to the grammar school in nearby Much Woolton (Woolton) in or

---

[13] From: Weekley, Ernest, *Romance of Names (1914)*, USA, Kessinger Publishing, 2003, p.97

around 1580. The school was approximately two miles from his home in South Allerton. An ancient school building, now a showpiece and used as a nursery, still exists in School Lane and the date etched in the sandstone over the door is 1610. This is too late for John Almond so it is possible that there was a school on the site before 1610 or the building may have been renovated. Men who were possibly involved with the school include Robert Quick, the 'schoolmaster' who wrote up the *Childwall Registers* in 1597–1598, and Edward Norris, of Speke, who died in 1606, left £60 in his will to provide a schoolmaster at Woolton. The Childwall register of 1557–1680 states:

> Here endeth the registering work of George Astley who hath been Schoolemaster of Muchwalton ten yeares and three quarters, and Register of Childwall parish three years and a halfe and upwards. He left the schoole May 5, 1657 and the Registers place May 9, 1657.[14]

It is believed that this school has not been used as such since the middle of the nineteenth century. The school buildings could be some of the oldest in the country.

JOHN'S STAY IN IRELAND

On the scaffold at Tyburn (now Marble Arch) in 1612, John told his accusers that, '[I] was about eight years old [when I] was carried over into Ireland, where [I] remained until [I] was at man's estate'[15] – doubtless to receive a Catholic education. One gathers that he was educated at one of the remaining religious houses or Catholic classical schools; he may have been tonsured by one of the Irish bishops. When John was interrogated at his trial before Bishop John King of London in 1612 he was asked if he had ever been abroad, and he said that he had been to Ireland. Bishop Richard Challoner, the author of *Memoirs of Missionary Priests*, said he must have been more than ten years abroad and the

---

[14] From: *Childwall Registers*, 1557–1680, p.18
[15] From a manuscript at Stonyhurst, quoted in: Steele, William J, *Blessed John Almond*, London, The Office of the Vice-Postulation, 1961, p.16

'old manuscript' affirms he employed the seas to improve himself in virtue and learning[16]. For the next thirteen years nothing whatsoever is recorded of him until he appeared in Rome in 1597. By secret routes Lancashire Catholics sent their sons to Douai, St Omer, Rome and elsewhere in Europe to be educated as priests, and from about 1575 the first trickle of Lancashire-born priests began to return to England. Ireland itself was no haven of peace in the 1580s. There had been continual rebellions suppressed with ferocity and, in 1586, at about the time of John's arrival, the Munster Plantation took place. Lands seized from the Irish were granted to the English settlers, and the Irish sank deeper into slavery and starvation. Sir William Pelham (1537–1587), who commanded the pioneers under the Duke of Norfolk, wrote to Queen Elizabeth:

> I keep [the rebels] from their harvest, and have taken great preys of cattle from them, by which it seemeth the poor people ... are so distressed as they follow their goods, and offer themselves, with their wives and children, rather to be slain by the army than to suffer the famine that now beginneth to pinch them.

In this unhappy country John Almond spent some of his boyhood.

JOHN ALMOND'S PARISH CHURCH

All Saints Church is Liverpool's most ancient parish church, with a Christian ministry stretching back over 900 years. A fourteenth-century document contains a reference to St Peter of Childwall[17], making it seem likely that the ancient dedication was to the Apostle Peter.

In 1094, Childwall became attached to the priory of Lancaster, a cell of the Abbey of St Martin at Seez in Normandy, and it remained so until the thirteenth century when the patronage passed to the Grelleys, barons of Manchester. In 1309, Sir Robert

---

[16] See: Challoner, *Memoirs of Missionary Priests*, p.329
[17] See: Mellor, E F, *This Our Heritage – All Saints Church, Childwall*, Childwall, All Saints Church, p.3

de Holland assigned Childwall to his college of secular canons at Upholland, near Wigan. Ten years later the endowments were assigned to the Benedictine monks at the new priory of St Thomas the Martyr at Upholland – Childwall was included among the endowments as a priory of Benedictine monks. By 1530, the priory had declined to two scholars and two aged and impotent folk, and complaints were made to the bishop about the extravagant lifestyle of the occupants. The patronage of Childwall belonged to the monks of the order until the dissolution of the monasteries by Henry VIII in 1536.

From 1557–1558 Childwall passed to the newly created See of Chester, carved out of Lichfield Diocese. The bishops were:

1556 – Cuthbert Scott

1561 – William Downham

1579 – William Chaderton

At present the patronage is vested in the See of Liverpool as it has been since its creation in 1880. The first bishop of Liverpool, John Charles Ryle, and his wife are both buried in Childwall churchyard and he is commemorated by a recumbent effigy within Liverpool cathedral designed by Charles Scott. The cathedral is one he only half-wished for, as his desire was originally to use the money to build more churches, not an expensive cathedral, as poverty was rife in Liverpool.

The earliest date that can be given to any part of the present church building is the fourteenth century, though there are fragments of earlier work built into the masonry from a later date. The fifteenth century saw the main part of the present parish church completed, and by the time of John Almond's baptism the building probably consisted of a west tower (with spire), chancel, nave, north and south aisles, south porch and north door.

An old method of commemorating the dead was to erect portraits executed in relief on metal – usually called 'brasses'. Some of the finest examples of these in the north of England are to be found in Childwall Parish Church, and are now situated in one of the alcoves in the south aisle. They commemorate Henry Norris of Speke Hall and his wife Clemence, who both died in the late sixteenth century. The chapel, on the south side of the church, is one of the oldest parts of the building. It is referred to in a document of 1484, and reads as follows:

> Thomas Norris of Speke, to the pleasure of God, encresse of His service, and for the helth of my sawle, and all myne antecessors, and for the helth of the sawle of John of Lathum, prieste, sumtyme parson of Aldeforth, and all cristen sawles founded a chantry in this chapel.[18]

This chapel was known as the chantry of St Thomas the Martyr; only the brasses remain. In 1563, the chapel had painted windows showing members of the Norris family. The general purpose of chantry chapels was for a daily celebration of Mass to take place therein for the benefit of the soul of some person or persons. The person who built the chapel would often be able to afford to establish an endowment to pay the priest, whose duty it was to see that the Mass was said daily. The Mass was often said for the soul of the person who had funded the building of the chapel. There are references to two such chapels – the Norris and one unknown.[19]

The earliest reference to the existence of a tower or steeple is found in the churchwardens' accounts for the year 1571, where there is a record that £15 was spent, 'chiffley upon leade about the stepell'[20]. Therefore, we cannot say in what year it was first built, only that it was probably sometime during the fourteenth century. There seems to have been bells in the tower for approximately five-hundred years, and in the centuries past their sound was so well-known and loved in the neighbourhood that an old rhyme mentions it as one of the distinctive features of Childwall:

> Prescot and Huyton and merry Childow,
> Three Parish Churches all in a row,
> Prescot for Poverty, Huyton for Pride,
> And Childwall for ringing and singing beside.[21]

---

[18] Mellor, *This Our Heritage – All Saints Church, Childwall*, Childwall, All Saints Church, p.9
[19] Ibid.
[20] Ibid., p.20
[21] Ibid., p.21

In 1517 it is recorded that three new bells were hung in the tower having been made by Richard Seliock of Nottingham. This is the first reference we have to the presence of bells, and after this time they appear quite frequently in the accounts. In 1552 there were only two bells, one having been sold in the meantime, but 1589 the number was once again restored to three. In the seventeenth-century records there are numerous references to the repair of the bells, and in 1666 we hear that the ringers rang with such vigour at the celebrations attending the restoration of Charles II in 1660 that the treble bell burst and had to be recast.[22]

There is another poem in the bell-ringers' chamber:

> If for to ring, a man comes here;
> Ringing sacred its Laws revere;
> These ringing Laws must be well us'd
> That ringers may not be abus'd;
> If ringer wears his spur or hat
> One quart of ale he pays for that;
> If while he rings, his bell o'er throw;
> Sixpence he pays before he go;
> But if he's heard to swear or curse;
> Demand one shilling of his Purse;
> If to these Laws he does conform
> The ringers part he may perform.[23]

In 1590 village churchwardens were not well regarded. Margaret Spufford says:

> Village churchwardens have been described as men of little (if any) wealth and status in their communities. They have been called the 'meanest and lewdest sort of people', men of 'humble origin' who 'seldom had any social standing or influence'.[24]

---

[22] Ibid., p.21
[23] Ibid., p.20
[24] From: Spufford, Margaret, *The World of Rural Dissenters 1520–1725*, Cambridge University Press, 1995, p.193

John Almond's Birth and Early Life, 1576–1597

A local Childwall verse described the duties of its sidesmen thus:

> To ken and see and say nowt
> To eat and drink and pay nowt;
> And when the wardens drunken roam
> Your duty is to see them home.[25]

During Queen Mary's reign – 1553–1558 (born 1516) – the last Catholic rector of Childwall was, appropriately, Richard Norris of Speke Hall. His successor, Rector William Crosse, is listed and had indeed been ordained a priest under Queen Mary, but it was the new Protestant bishop of Chester, William Downham (1561), who appointed him to Childwall circa 1562. However, after a brief temporising, the Crosse family returned to the Catholic faith and William Crosse resigned in 1569. He was followed by David Calton in 1569/70 who was rector at the time of John Almond's christening. In 1588, Lawrence Blackborne became rector, followed the year after by Thomas Williamson in 1589 and then Edmund Hapwood, also in 1589.

So long established was the Norris interest in the welfare of Childwall village that they continued to be churchwardens in spite of their recusancy. Jane, William and Elizabeth Norris are listed in the Recusant Rolls of 1593–1594.

> Jane Norres, lately of Speake (Speke); William Norres, lately of Speake; Elizabeth Norres, wife of the said William. [Each were fined] £140 for the like ... Enrolments of estreated convictions for recusancy.[26]

Many others are listed in the hundred of West Derby, including Alice Almond, lately of Allerton in the Parish of Childwall and a widow. The hundred of West Derby was an ancient division of the historic county of Lancashire as seen on the following page.

The churchwardens' accounts from 1590–1634 show that some of the villagers who had conformed, though not having to pay the crushing recusancy fines exacted from their stronger brethren, did not always get off scot-free: two men were fined for piping in the churchyard during sermon time, others for gossip-

---

[25] From: Tindal Hart, Arthur, *The Man in the Pew 1558–1660*, UK, Baker, 1966
[26] From: Bowler, *Recusant Rolls No 2 1593–1594*, p.84

ing in the churchyard or even in the church itself during and others again for 'usually sleeping' in church during the sermons.

Numerous offenders were sentenced and admonished for acts such as haunting the ale houses at service time and not bringing the children to be catechised. They were dealt with severely.

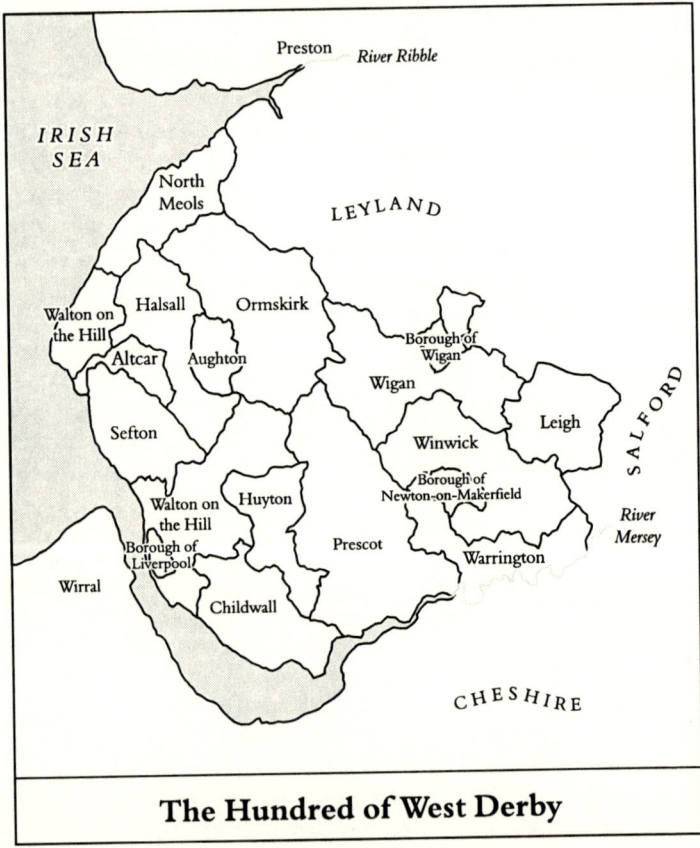

The Hundred of West Derby

THE PARISH OF CHILDWALL

The earliest reference to Childwall (Cildevelle) is found in the Domesday Book of 1086. A reproduction of the entry concerning 'Cildevelle' in the Domesday Book is inscribed on the wall beside

John Almond's Birth and Early Life, 1576–1597

the churchwardens' pew at Childwall Parish Church. There was probably a chapel and a priest there in the eleventh century and an extract from the Domesday Book reads:

> Four Radmans held Childewall as four manors. There is half a hide. It is worth eight shillings. There was a priest, having half a carucate of land in frank almoign.

Neither a hide nor a carucate is a measure of area – both are units of work, which could be performed in a certain time. A carucate was a measure of land varying with the nature of the soil etc., being as much as could be tilled with one plough – with its team of eight oxen – in a year. In Lancashire, as Domesday itself says, there were six carucates to one hide. Two carucates represent sixteen oxen – two plough teams.

Few people were wealthy enough to own a whole team and, just as cooperation in sowing and harvesting was necessary in villages with open fields, so cooperation in putting together plough teams was essential to good husbandry. The population that could live from the two carucates would have been a few dozen. 'Frank almoign' may be translated as 'free alms'.

In addition to the township that gives name to the parish, there are in Childwall eight other townships – Much Woolton, Little Woolton, Hale, Halewood, Speke, Garston, Allerton and Wavertree.

No church existed in Allerton until 1872. The parish church of Childwall, two or three miles away, sufficed till then for the spiritual needs of the few inhabitants of Allerton. Many Allerton families from very early days possessed a pew at Childwall.

The Childwall Cross has often been associated with monks who are believed to have lived in Childwall Abbey or Childwall Priory. In fact there has never been an abbey or a priory at Childwall. The origin of the 'abbey legend' lies in the fact that the first owners of Childwall Old Hall were of a romantic turn of mind and named their abode Childwall Abbey. The priory was a farmhouse which stood where the busy thoroughfare of Childwall fiveways is now. The stories of massacres at the time of King Henry VIII's dissolution of the monasteries, of monks and of secret passages between the abbey and the priory must belong only to the world of fable and imagination. The only real connection that Childwall has with monastic life, as previously mentioned, is that the patronage of the living was for many years in the hands of the Benedictine monks of Upholland and Childwall and neighbouring Woolton were overseen by a Benedictine mission.

The Parish of Prescot

Three miles across the valley from Childwall and eight miles away from the centre of Liverpool stands the parish church of Prescot. At the time of John Almond, this would have been visible from Childwall as there were no tower blocks or motorways interrupting the view. Prescot church occupies a site of extreme antiquity upon the southern brow on the crest of a hill 300 feet above sea level, commanding an extensive prospect, and in former times was thickly wooded, being the most prominent object for miles around. Just past the church lies Wood Lane which continues down the hill to Carr Lane – the locals refer to it as 'The Woodies'. Knowsley Hall stands in Knowsley Park and is the principal seat of Lord Derby. It adjoins the boundary of Prescot and St Helens, only four miles away. The parish church of St Mary's Prescot was dedicated to All Saints in ancient times, a fact which suggests a very early origin. The present building is said to be the fourth church on the site since the eleventh century but there is strong reason to believe that there was a place of worship there many centuries before that time. Indeed, there is good reason to believe that this spot was a religious sanctuary even in pre-Christian times. Furthermore, in the days before the English settled in these parts, it is probable that Celtic missionary monks – brethren of the saintly Patrick, Columba, Aidan and Cuthbert – built a plain Christian church of timber and clay. The hill site and circular churchyard suggest Celtic origins.

All Saints Parish Church was rededicated, probably when reconstructed in 1610 (two years before the death of John Almond in 1612), to St Mary the Virgin. Little is known of the preceding church, which in 1555 had been reported as having:

John Almond's Birth and Early Life, 1576–1597

...so great ruins and deformities and dilapidation's in the roofs, ornaments, walls and windows that, unless speedy remedy be taken, the said church is in a short time likely to fall down to the ground.[27]

The church founded two grammar schools in the parish: one during the reign of Henry VIII at Farnworth in 1507, and one during the reign of Elizabeth I at Prescot in 1544. These Tudor schools were called grammar schools because their curriculum was based upon the study of Latin grammar.

Prescot lay just to the west of that mysterious 'boundary line' dividing old Catholic south-west Lancashire from the industrialising pastoral regions of enthusiastic Puritanism spreading westwards from Manchester and Bolton. Ancient Prescot was very extensive, comprising of fifteen townships making a total area of 37,221 acres.

The land workers of the hundred of West Derby were mostly recusant and Catholicism was sustained in an almost seigniory form. Prescot had been slow in enforcing the reformation changes of the previous century and in 1604 shared with Huyton, Childwall, Wigan and Eccleston a reputation as one of the most Catholic parishes in Lancashire. The heads of households in the parishes were styled gent – as gentlemen – in the 1630s, and were almost all recusant or church papists.

In the seventeenth century considerable political and religious importance was attached to the ecclesiastical unit – the parish. For example, the ancient parish of Prescot lay in the rural deanery of Warrington in the Diocese of Chester (previously Lichfield) and covered some fifty-eight square miles in all, 37,221 acres of the hundred of West Derby and embraced fifteen townships. On the north or 'Prescot side' of the parish were the eight townships of Eccleston, Parr, Prescot, Rainford, Rainhill, Sutton, Whiston and Windle; and on the south, or 'Farnworth side' the seven further townships of Bold, Cronton, Cuerdley, Ditton, Great Sankey, Penketh and Widnes cum Appleton. The parish included the sites of the modern

---

[27] Bailey, F A, *Prescot Parish Church – Official Guide*, Gloucester, The British Publishing Company, p.5

towns of Widnes and St Helens and much of the western side of Warrington within its boundaries.

The Mersey and the parishes of Childwall, Huyton, Walton, Ormskirk, Wigan, Winwick and Warrington were in the Deanery of Warrington. Obviously such sprawling parishes could not be served by one church alone. Even the staunchest churchgoer would have been daunted by the long ride on horseback to their parish church, particularly in bad weather when the lanes were quagmires. In most villages the only public meeting places were the church and the alehouses, and only the church would contain all the villagers. The great distances that some of the parishioners had to travel to their church made it necessary to provide subsidiary places of worship in the more distant parts of the parish. It was to serve the needs of the outlying parts of the parish that auxiliary 'chapels-of-ease' were built – a term which has nothing to do with comfort but is simply a reference to ease of travel.

Catholics in South-west Lancashire

Lancashire was the strongest Catholic county in England from 1567 onwards, especially after the Reformation and particularly in Ribblesdale, the Fylde and the south-west. For very good reasons, our Catholic forefathers were reticent. Lancashire was recognised by the enemies of the Catholic Church as its greatest stronghold, particularly among the influential landowners. Many landed gentry even refused to attend their parish church. They were called recusants – those who refused to go to church. They encouraged their tenants to follow their example. For security reasons, Catholics trained themselves to play down their own strength. They dispensed with written records for fear that it may lead to further persecution.

The oldest surviving religious site in the town of St Helens is the ruined Catholic Windleshaw chantry, dedicated to St Thomas and today standing within the borough cemetery. Sir Thomas Gerard of Bryn of Windle Hall in St Helens built this structure in 1453 to provide a place to celebrate Mass for the souls of the Gerard family. It remained in use and good order through to the sixteenth century, when King Henry VIII's commissioners during the period of the dissolution of the monastic houses visited it. Though being of lowly stature compared to the priories and abbeys, it is not recorded as to what was found there. In 1627, the enclosed graveyard was used as a secret burial ground by the local recusant Catholic community, with the dead being buried there in the dark of night. On Easter Monday 2008, a Mass was celebrated after 450 years in this historic chantry.

Sir Thomas' son, John, was one of the most fascinating of the Jesuit priests. Sir Thomas was imprisoned in the Tower of

London when John was five years old for plotting the rescue of Mary, Queen of Scots. At the age of fourteen, John attended the Douai seminary at Rheims, where he decided to enter the Society of Jesus. He returned to England in foreign clothing but was soon arrested in Dover. He was sent to London's Marshalea Prison, where many undercover priests had been imprisoned. He then went to Rome and was given another mission on behalf of the Jesuits which sent him to England. In November 1588, three months after the defeat of the Spanish Armada he landed in Norfolk. On this mission he was caught in London, was tried and found guilty. He was imprisoned in the Counter in the Poultry and moved to the Clink. Eventually because of his continued mission he was sent to the Salt Tower in the Tower of London, where he was further questioned and tortured by being repeatedly suspended from chains on the dungeon wall. The files in the tower say he never broke under torture. After his experiences of torture, John went into hiding in London. He realised that he was such a wanted man that he had no choice but to flee the country. He crossed over to the continent dressed in livery in the entourage of the ambassadors of Flanders and Spain, where he lived the rest of his life relatively quietly.

 Lord Burghley's Map of Lancashire

In about 1590, William Cecil, Lord Burghley, had a map of Lancashire drawn so that, by seeing the relative position of gentlemen's houses, he could more easily take precautionary measures against Catholics and easily note the names of the principal Catholic families. On this map an X marked those who were considered to need special coercion to make them conform to the new Protestant religion.

Changes in religion happened slowly in Lancashire due to the poor state of the roads, marshes, peat bogs and heaths making travelling difficult. Roads were little more than rutted tracks, which varied in width according to the weather. The wetter it was, the wider the track, as people and animals tried to avoid the churned-up mud in the centre. The local parishes, who were supposed to be responsible for the upkeep of roads, would occasionally fill in the holes when they got too bad, using whatever materials were to hand at least expense. Bridges, however, were of greater importance; their maintenance was vital and therefore the responsibility of the Court of Quarter Sessions. Even the lord of the manor was answerable for their upkeep.

In 1585 Queen Elizabeth's government considered that, despite several arrests, there were still over a score of priests secretly active in Lancashire. The war with Spain increased anxiety, for the government feared Spanish landing on the Lancashire coast.

The Bishop of Chester (1579–1595), William Chaderton, reported to the Privy Council in 1590 that, 'The number of

Saint John Almond and the Society of his Time

recusants is great and doth dailie increase'[28]. He visited southwest Lancashire in 1592.

In 1590 seven-hundred Lancashire recusants were brought before the justices and 'yet the number doubted to be far greater'[29]. Some were imprisoned, others fined, but these punishments did not reduce the number of Catholics in Lancashire. In 1641, John Pym (1584–1643), Parliamentarian and one of the five members whom Charles I attempted to arrest in 1642, declared in the Commons that there were 1,800 Lancashire recusants. However, official figures in 1667 gave 5,496 for Lancashire, 1,855 for Yorkshire, 96 for Essex and only 52 for London and Middlesex.

---

[28] From: Barker, T C and Newbury, N F, *The Growth of St Helens – A Preliminary Survey*, St Helens Library & Education Committee, 1940, p.8

[29] From: Bagley, J J, *A History of Lancashire*, Phillimore & Co, Ltd, UK, 1976, p.55

John Almond's World

THE SECRET CHAPELS OF SOUTH-WEST LANCASHIRE

From the old ferry terminal at Liverpool, there were fifty or more secret chapels that could be reached by horse within a day (see map on p.41). Seven halls or secret chapels were situated in what is now the City of Liverpool: Croxteth Hall, Childwall Hall, Woolton Hall, Allerton Hall, Aigburth Hall, Garston Hall and Speke Hall. John Almond's childhood home on the borders of Allerton and Speke would have been within easy walking distance of six of these: Childwall, Woolton, Allerton, Aigburth, Garston and Speke. He must have been a regular visitor to some of these.

For at least two hundred years, Catholic village life centred on the hall of the Lord of the Manor. Very often, a distinguished priest lived there, or at least visited from time to time, providing Mass for the faithful Catholics. Celebrating the Mass was always a drama, wondering when the next visit of government spies (pursuivants) would take place. Almost all these halls had secret hiding places for the priest to live in and a lookout would always be to hand when the service took place.

AIGBURTH HALL

The thirteenth-century hall buildings were divided when the present Aigburth Hall Avenue was built. Little remains of the original, which has been constantly changed over the years. It now appears as a small, sandstone structure. The hall was quite near to the banks of the Mersey between the Liverpool ferry and Speke Hall. It was a Cistercian grange of Whalley Abbey near Stonyhurst, the Jesuit school in North Lancashire.

> It is likely ... there are graves of a Jesuit and another priest, because inscriptions are carved into the old sandstone wall that read: 'I.D., 1765' and 'I.B., I.H.S.' (I.H.S is the emblem of the Society of Jesus). Priests could not, of course, be buried publicly in cemeteries, but only under cover of darkness in some secret spot in or near a chapel.[30]

John Almond's home would have been one and a half miles away from this hall and he would probably have received the sacrament there.

ALLERTON HALL

This hall was only a mile and a half east of Aigburth. The great Lathom family owned this between the twelfth and seventeenth centuries. The Lathom family also owned Lathom, Knowsley, Huyton and Tarbock. These were then owned by the famous Stanley family. The Lathom family is listed in the Lancashire recusancy rolls. A number of priests were produced from the village including John Almond (Amott) alias Lathom, alias Molyneux. The Lord of the Manor at the time of his childhood was Thomas Lathom of Parbold.

The 1627 inventory of Mistress Lathom's effects give a picture of a small house. This consisted of an entrance hall which also served as the chief living room, a dining room, two or three bedrooms, a servant's room, storerooms, larders and a brew house. The house was rebuilt in 1659. Allerton had been a village of few inhabitants for many years, consisting of the hall and a few poor farm cottages. Only fifteen tenants are mentioned in the Manorial Deeds of 1653–1654. One of these was Susanna Almond (a Susan Almond of Allerton was married to John Broughton of Much Woolton on 5 November 1658).[31]

---

[30] From: Stonor, *Liverpool's Hidden Story*, p.37
[31] From: *Childwall Registers*, 1557–1680

CHILDWALL HALL

Nothing much is recorded about this hall or its occupants. The first owners named their abode 'Childwall Abbey', a romantic version of the name, but that hall is now demolished. Stonor, in *Liverpool's Hidden Story* lists it as being sold to a Protestant purchaser in 1718 and later demolished.[32] Derek Whale refers in his book to the major ancient Childwall residence, a large, castellated and turreted building in sandstone, built in 1780 for Bamber Gascoyne, MP for Truro. Bamber Gascoyne of television's *University Challenge* is related![33]

GARSTON HALL

Garston is one of the eight townships forming the parish of Childwall. The first recorded mention of settlement is the church of St Michael in 1235. In medieval times, until the time of the suppression of the monasteries, it was home to a group of Benedictine monks. They belonged to the Benedictines of Upholland Priory, Lancashire. The hall, erected in about 1480, was a half-timbered, H-shaped building.

In a field below the mill, a scourge of seven chains was found. This presumably belonged to the monks as such chains were used as a severe form of self-inflicted discipline administered during the recitation of the seven penitential psalms. The chain found near Garston was fitted with spikes, instead of the usual chain which had leather thongs or cord.[34]

It is probable that a priest from Speke Hall would come to Garston to celebrate the Mass. Records suggest that in Elizabethan times there were very few Protestants in the village.

---

[32] Stonor, *Liverpool's Hidden Story*, p.48
[33] Whale, Derek, *Lost Villages of Liverpool – Part 3*, second edition, T Stephenson and Sons Ltd., Prescot, Merseyside
[34] Stonor, *Liverpool's Hidden Story*, p.67

Speke Hall

The hall is one of a small number of surviving large, timber-framed manor houses in the north-west of England built in the medieval and Tudor period. A visit I made to the house demonstrated to me that it is one of the most perfectly preserved timbered buildings in the country. Credit for this must be given to the National Trust and to Merseyside County Council who resumed responsibility for the hall in 1974.

Major structural and restoration work has been carried out by Merseyside City Council with help from the Historic Buildings Council. There have been no major alterations or additions to this Tudor gentry's family house. Large numbers of people visit the hall, probably with many not realising the part in once played in history.

The house stands between the River Mersey and John Lennon airport. It was built between the fifteenth and early seventeenth centuries by the Norris family. They were important landowners in south Lancashire and Cheshire. They resided there until the mid-eighteenth century. The hall was in the Parish of Childwall and only two miles from Allerton, the birthplace of John Almond. As recusants, John's family probably visited the hall frequently for their Mass.

The Norrises clung to the old Catholic faith and used their home for sheltering priests when they had entered or were leaving the still largely Catholic area of south-west Lancashire.

In 1598 it was reported that ' "Little Sir Richard" and "Sir Peter" for the most parte lodged in a chamber over the parlour'.[35] The hall was strategically placed on the banks of the River Mersey, as the sheriffs' powers only extended to the borders of the county that they oversaw. Many wealthy Catholics kept a second home in a different county, with their residences being placed on a county border. On the north-west corner of Lancashire, a priest-hunter complained:

> If search be made in Lancashire, upon an hour's warning they will be in Westmoreland, and if search be made there, upon

---
[35] Ibid., p.90

another hour's warning they will be in Cumberland. With approximately three of four hours, they may be conveyed by land into Scotland or the Isle of Man.[36]

Edward Norris, between 1568–1598, built more hiding places for priests with spy holes and views to the lodge. They had their own fishermen on the rivers Mersey and Dee and when it was dusk they could transport priests in secret on their way to other 'safe houses'.

In 1590, Lord Burghley understandably put a cross against Edward Norris of Speke on his map of recusant Lancashire and his wife, too, was described as a 'notorious recusant'.[37] All Edward Norris' children were christened, married and buried 'with Masses and Romish ceremonies'.[38]

WOOLTON HALL

In 1189, John Constable of Chester granted a charge to the religious order of St John of Jerusalem. For 350 years, they held lands in Woolton until it was confiscated in 1559 by Queen Elizabeth I. The manorial rights then passed from her to James I who then sold them to William Stanley, sixth Earl of Derby. The Molyneux family had the hall built in 1704. In 1772, Robert Adams was employed to design a new frontage and redesign the interior.

The marriage of William Brettargh of Woolton to the Puritan, Katherine Bruen, sister of John Bruen of Stapleford, a famous Puritan, caused much fanatical hatred against the Catholic population.

The preacher at the funeral of Katherine drew blood-curdling pictures of the 'inhuman bands of brutish Papists' among whom she had had to live, since 'Popish recusants, Church papists, profane atheists and carnal Protestants swarm together like hornets in these parts'. The only recorded injury she suffered was when the Norris family of Speke Hall impounded some of her

---

[36] Ibid.
[37] Ibid.
[38] Ibid.

cattle that had strayed onto their land, but on that occasion the Bishop of Chester wrote to the queen:

> We commend the barbarous facts to your favour, from which only we may expect reformation of these outrages of late committed by Catholics, not without the designments of pestilential seminaries [i.e. priests] that lurk among them.[39]

William Brettargh himself wrote that, 'If her Majesty should grant any toleration to the papists, she would not be worthy to be queen'. The Catholics were at least more tolerant, for William Blundell of Crosby described Katherine Brettargh's son, Nehemiah, who drank himself to death (and it is hard to sympathise with him), as 'an honest good fellow'[40].

Some of the other halls and secret chapels around Liverpool included:

Alt Grange	Hall I' th' Wood, Melling	Ravenhead Hall
Appleton		St Winifred's Well, Holywell
Aughton Hall	Halsnead, Whiston	
Birchley Hall	Hardshaw Hall	Scholes Hall
Bold Hall	Hooton Hall	Sutton Hall
Crank Hall	Huyton Hey	Tarbock Hall
Crosby Hall	Ince Blundell Hall and New House	The Hutte
Croxteh Hall and Gillmoss		Thurstaston Hall
	Lydiate Hall	Tuebrook House
Ditton Hall	Maghull Hall	Whiston Hall
Eccleston Hall	Moor Hall	Widnes
Fazakerlet Hall and Spellow House	Mossborough Hall	Windle Hall
	Mossock Hall	Wolfall Hall
Aintree House and Tatlock House, Formby	Parr Hall	
	Poole Hall	
	Puddington Hall	
Gerard Hall	Rainhill Hall	

---

[39] Ibid., p.104
[40] Ibid.

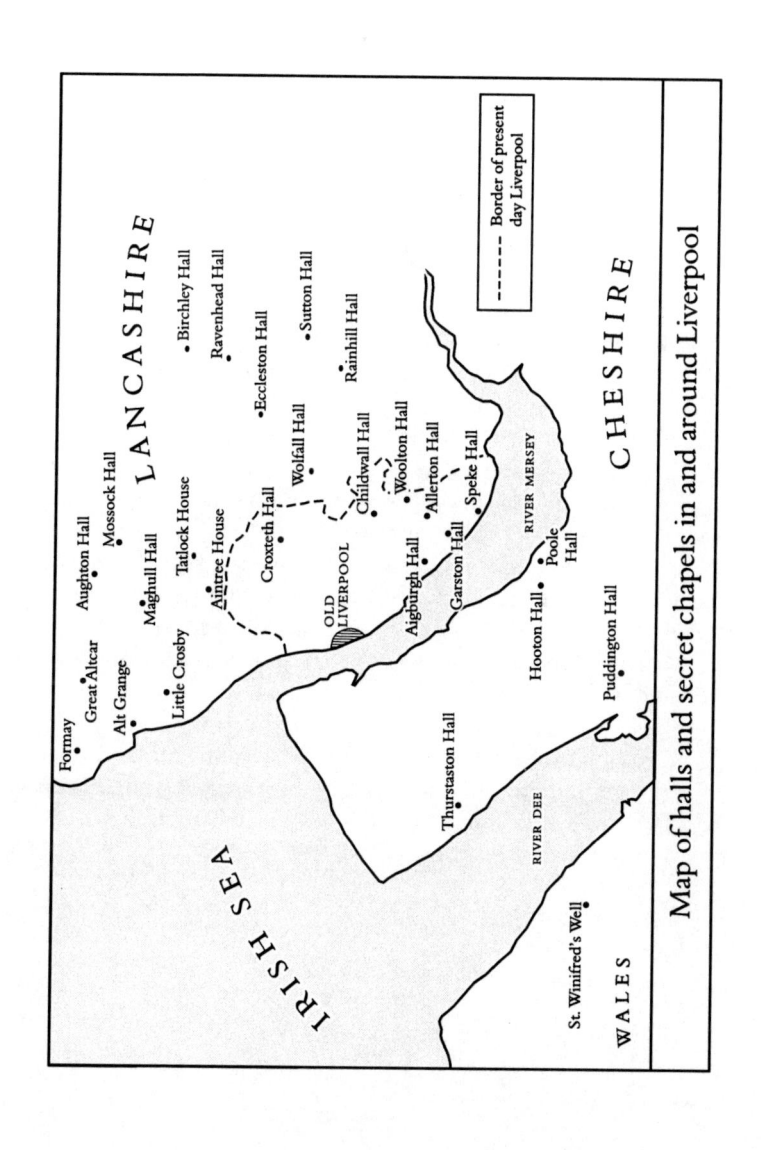

Map of halls and secret chapels in and around Liverpool

The River Mersey – Birkenhead to Liverpool Ferry

The banks of the River Mersey are at their nearest point between Liverpool and Birkenhead, both points having a natural pool and harbour. Naturally, this was the best place for a ferry, which would cut a whole day's riding between Chester, North Wales and Lancashire. Although not yet ports, large numbers of travellers crossed over this stretch of water less than a mile wide by the hospitality of the monks of Birkenhead Priory.

The Benedictine Priory was founded between 1155 and 1160. In 1318, the monks from Birkenhead were granted ferry rights by Edward II. They built a house to store their corn and this was also used by travellers for shelter if the weather was too bad for the ferry to cross the River Mersey.

Hospitality to the travellers was an important part of the monks' lifestyle. By 1330, charity could not fully cover the costs of the monks' hospitality and they were given a royal licence to charge a fee to those who used the ferry. The charge was a farthing for a man and twopence for a man and horse, since the horse occupied the space of seven men, but only a halfpenny for a man and horse on a Saturday, which was the market day in Liverpool.

The 'Monks' Ferry' is still the official name of the priory landing stage and the fact that the ferry dues are still paid only on the Birkenhead side is another reminder of what had been, for almost four hundred years, a great work of charity.[41]

---

[41] Ibid., p.3

Contemporary People and Events in and Around the Time of John Almond

The following notable people and events give us a better understanding of the world John Almond lived in.

ST MARGARET CLITHEROW OF YORK, 1556–1586

Nearly four-hundred years after her martyrdom, on 25 October 1970, Margaret was declared a saint and one of the forty martyrs of England and Wales.

Margaret was the daughter of Thomas Middleton, a candle maker, born in 1556 – the fourth year of the reign of Queen Mary. Margaret was baptised in the parish church of St Martin-le-Grand, Coney Street, York, where her father was churchwarden. On the accession of Queen Mary he had been responsible for restoring the old Catholic services. When, on the death of Queen Mary, yet another change of religion was introduced, he went along with it. As a child, Margaret was brought up as a Protestant.

In 1571, when she was only fifteen, she married John Clitherow, a retail butcher in the Shambles, York – then a narrow, smelly street that was used as an abattoir. There is still a butcher in the Shambles today and there is also a shrine to St Margaret. A year after his marriage, John was sworn in as a special constable to assist the hunting down of Catholic suspects. This was the year in which Margaret became a Catholic. It seems that her husband remained indifferent to his wife's religion.

In 1576, the first priests from Douai reached England; several were found sheltering in the Clitherow home. Soon, Margaret became a marked woman. Between 1577 and 1584 she was sent to prison several times. It must be borne in mind that Catholics under Queen Elizabeth were persecuted as Protestants had been under Mary. Margaret set up a Mass room in the city but at that time, with the arrival of the first Jesuit priests in 1580, the persecution had become more severe.

Between July 1582 and May 1583 five priests were captured and executed at Knavesmire, York on the banks of the River Ouse. Margaret was now under constant observation as she visited the gallows. In 1583 she was again in prison, this time for eighteen months. As a notorious shelterer of priests, her home in the Shambles was raided on 12 March 1586 and she was arrested. She was put on trial. The charge was that she had harboured and maintained Jesuit and seminary priests, traitors to the Queen's Majesty and her laws, that she had heard Mass and suchlike.

Margaret refused to plead. The penalty for not pleading was to be pressed to death. For the next ten days she remained in prison. After this time the sheriffs took her to the toll booth by the river, a few yards from the prison, where she was permitted to kneel in prayer. She was then laid naked on her back for three days without food or drink, except a little barley bread and puddle water. On the third day, her hands and feet were tied to posts and a sharp stone was placed under her back. As the weights were laid on her she said, 'Jesu, Jesu, Jesu, have mercy on me.' Within a quarter of an hour she was dead.

ROBERT MIDDLETON, 1570–1601

A seminary priest and Jesuit, Robert Middleton was born at York in 1570; the son of Thomas Middleton and a nephew of Margaret Clitherow (née Middleton). He was educated until he was eighteen at St Peter's School, York, possibly with Guy Fawkes, during which time 'he thinketh he did usually go to church'[42]. He then refused to go but could not tell who persuaded him therefrom, other than his own conscience and the reading of books. The next six or seven years were spent in London and at the

---

[42] Anstruther, G O P, *The Seminary Priests –Volume 1*, Durham, St Edmund's College, 1968, p.230

house in Kingston-upon-Hull of Mr Richardson, a merchant and alderman of that town. He crossed from Hull to Calais in a ship of Newcastle laden with coals, and spent three years at Douai. The names of his fellow students were not recorded. He was then sent to the English College, Rome with John Almond on 14 April 1597. He was ordained at the German College on 4 January 1598 and sent to England on 20 April 1598. On 8 November, Robert was one of the seventy-nine priests who petitioned for the appointment of an archpriest. Lord Burghley first captured him in a house at Ripon, Yorkshire at Christmas 1599 together with Martin Nelson. Burghley called Robert a 'very stout and resolute fellow'[43]. Somehow Robert regained his freedom, only to be taken again on 30 September 1600 by Sir Richard Houghton in the Fylde, on the highway. On 1 October he was imprisoned at Preston. The next day the mayor of Preston and an armed guard escorted him to Lancaster Castle. There was a desperate effort to rescue him by a priest, Thurstan Hunt and three lay Catholics at Haworth Moor, near Garstang, Lancashire. The Privy Council was notified and both priests were ordered on 8 November 1600 to the Gatehouse, London. During his imprisonment, Middleton was admitted to the Society of Jesus. On 1 March 1601 the council sent detailed instructions for the return journey – they were to travel with their feet tied under the horse's belly. Further instructions were given on 3 March. They were condemned at the next assizes, held at Lancaster, and martyred there together in March 1601 for priesthood. They were hanged, drawn and quartered.

WILLIAM SHAKESPEARE, 1564–1616

Stratford's most famous son was born of a glover and, in 1582, he married Anne Hathaway, who bore him three children. He was undoubtedly England's greatest poet and dramatist. He was grammar-school educated, and became an actor, having been raised in Stratford-upon-Avon and making his career in London. He is known to have been active in the London theatre by 1592.

---

[43] Ibid., p.231

His works, translated and performed throughout the world, have made him the most celebrated and most quoted English writer. He was very popular in his day; his plays were put on for the entertainment of everyone – not merely for the 'educated'.

William Shakespeare had connections to the Catholics on the periphery of the Gunpowder Plot and *Macbeth* contains allusions to the fate of the 'equivocating' Jesuit, Henry Garnet.

WILLIAM SHAKESPEARE AND KNOWSLEY

The first purpose-built indoor theatre in Britain (the Playhouse) was in Prescot (Lancashire) in the 1590s. The location of this original Elizabethan theatre in Prescot and the wider Borough of Knowsley have a particularly rich history.

Academic research has now indicated that William Shakespeare spent the early part of his career (the 'lost years' in the late 1570s and 1580s before he went to London) in Lancashire in the service of wealthy and influential families – the Hoghtons, the Heskeths and the Stanleys.

The Earls of Derby (the Stanleys) were one of the most influential families in England, living in Knowsley Hall. Lord Strange (fifth Earl of Derby) and his brother William (sixth Earl) were directly involved in theatre, maintaining a particularly talented troupe of professional players called 'Strange's Men'. This company of players included Thomas Pope, Will Kempe and John Hemmings, who later formed the core of the Chamberlain's Men with Shakespeare at the Globe in London. The likelihood is that William Shakespeare first encountered these players while in the service of Ferdinando Stanley at Knowsley Hall. In *Love's Labours Lost*, King Ferdinand's ambition to make his court the wonder of the world is likely to have been based on the real plans of Ferdinando Stanley. Had he lived longer, Ferdinando Stanley would have been the leading English contender for the throne. Shakespeare almost certainly wrote his early plays while under the patronage of these powerful Lancashire families. Evidence from archival records is supported by references in the plays.

There is evidence that some of Shakespeare's earliest plays such as *Richard III* and *Love's Labours Lost*, which contain tributes to the Stanleys, were first staged in Prescot or at Knowsley Hall. If so, William Shakespeare would almost certainly have supervised the performances – and may even have acted in them.

GUY FAWKES, 1570–1606

Guy Fawkes is easily the best remembered participant in the conspiracy known as the Gunpowder Plot, the aim of which was to blow up the Houses of Parliament while King James I and his chief ministers met within. This was in reprisal for increasing oppression of Catholics in England.

Fawkes was a member of a prominent York family. His father was Edward and his mother was Edith Blake-Jacksonne. He was born on 13 April 1570 in York and married Maria Pulleyn of Scotton in or around 1590. When he was eight his father died and two or three years later his mother married a recusant, Denis Bainbridge. Their life at Scotton near Knaresborough brought Guy formally into the Yorkshire Catholic orbit. The earliest strong Catholic influence upon Guy Fawkes was, however, exerted by St Peter's School, York. The school building still stands and is in use as a school. It is claimed to be the oldest in the country. His schoolfellows included three men who became priests: Oswald Tesimond, Edward Olcorne and Robert Middleton. Fawkes adventurous spirit as well as his religious zeal led him to leave Protestant England in 1593 and enlist in the Spanish army in the Netherlands. There he won a reputation for great courage and cool determination. Meanwhile, the instigator of the plot, Robert Catesby, and his small band of Catholics agreed that they needed the help of a military man who would not be readily recognisable as they were. They dispatched a man to the Netherlands in April 1604 to enlist Fawkes, who, without knowing the precise details of the plot, returned to England and joined them. He changed his name to Guido Fawkes, the name he also used for his official signature. He thought of himself as a sincere Catholic and patriotic Englishman – an Englishman abroad but with the true interests of his country at heart.

Gunpowder Plot

In 1605 a group of Catholic hotheads, men of good families, plotted to blow up Parliament at the very moment it was being opened by the king. They rented a cellar extending under Parliament, and Fawkes planted at least twenty barrels of gunpowder there, camouflaged with coals and faggots. In one huge explosion the Lords and Commons and most of the royal family were to have been wiped out; then one of the king's children was to be put on the throne and married to a foreign Catholic prince. They arranged to have a fifteen-minute time fuse lit by Guy Fawkes so that the explosion happened while King James I and both houses were together for the ceremonial opening. They came close to achieving this. However, the plot was discovered. Lord Monteagle, a Catholic peer, received an anonymous letter warning him to keep away and he showed it to Lord Edward Cecil. Fawkes was duly arrested on 4 November, caught in the act. Only after being tortured did he reveal the name of his accomplices. Tried and found guilty before a special commission on 27 January 1606, he was executed opposite the Parliament building where the others confessed to their treason and were also executed after being tried.

John Donne, 1572–1631

An English poet and Anglican divine of Welsh extraction, John Donne came from a devout Catholic family but renounced his faith in his early twenties. Of his own Catholic upbringing in London he said:

> I had my first breeding and conversation with men of a suppressed and afflicted religion, accustomed to the despite of death and hungry of an imagined martyrdom.[44]

His mother was the sister of the Jesuit missionary priest called Jasper Heywood, and a granddaughter of a sister of Thomas Moore (one-time Lord Chancellor of England).

---

[44] Donne, John, Preface to *Biathanatos*

He sailed with the Earl of Essex and with Sir Walter Raleigh on expeditions against Spain, which are described in his poems 'The Storm' and 'The Calm'. After serving various noble patrons, Donne apostatised, joined the Anglican ministry in 1615 under the instruction of King James and ended his days from 1621 as Dean of St Paul's, still uncertain where to find the true Church of Christ and still tortured by doubt. He wrote a stirring sonnet as late as 1617 called 'Show me, deare Christ, thy spouse so bright and clear.' He was a celebrated preacher and his later work was mainly religious: 'Holy Sonnets' and 'Hymns'; the prose *Devotions* and the sermons which include the famous 'Death Duel', delivered shortly before his death

THE ARMADA – 1588

When John Almond was about eleven years old, a large naval and military force was sent by Philip II of Spain to invade England at the end of May 1588. It consisted of 130 ships carrying about 8,000 sailors and 19,000 infantrymen under the command of the inexperienced Duke of Medina Sidonia. The Spanish fleet was delayed by a storm off Corunna, and was first sighted by the English naval commanders on 19 July, then harassed by them with long-range guns, until it anchored off Calais. Unable to liase with an additional force from the low countries led by Farnese, its formation was wrecked by English fireships during the night and, as it tried to escape, it suffered a further pounding from the English fleet before a strong wind drove the remaining vessels into the North Sea and they were forced to make their way back to Spain round the north of Scotland and the west of Ireland. Barely half of the original Armada returned to port.

BRITISH HANGING

In antiquity, hanging was considered a form of death befitting cowards. Consequently, it was seen as a dishonourable way to die. In England, from Anglo-Saxon times it was the traditional method of execution, until William the Conqueror introduced beheading in the eleventh century. Although executions were carried out throughout the country, the most usual place for the public execution of common criminals became Jack Ketch's tree at Tyburn in London, though there were also gallows elsewhere in London: in Soho Square, Bloomsbury Square, Smithfield, St Giles in Holborn and Blackheath, and on Kensington Common and City Road in Islington. Occasionally people were publicly hanged outside the place where they had committed a particularly heinous crime.

The place of execution was known as Tyburn Fields, a large area of rough ground through which the River Ty flowed ('burn' means 'river' or 'stream' in Old English). A stand of elm trees grew on the banks of the Ty and the Normans considered the elm to be the 'tree of justice'. At least 50,000 people met a violent death on this 'tree of justice' at Tyburn between 1196 and 1783, the year of the last execution.

Queen Elizabeth I, 1533–1603

Elizabeth was born on 7 September 1533 – the illegitimate daughter of King Henry VIII and Anne Boleyn. She reigned from 1559 until her death on 24 March 1603. John Almond was born in the twentieth year of her reign. She never married and some referred to her as The Virgin Queen. Others named her Gloriana or Good Queen Bess. Her long reign was marked by turmoil.

In 1559, the Act of Supremacy made it high treason in England to take notice of the pope's authority. The queen was to be acknowledged as Supreme Governor of the Church and State. The Act of Uniformity in the same year restored the Book of Common Prayer, introduced in 1549 by Edward VI and then withdrawn by Queen Mary. This Act of Uniformity prohibited the Mass and made attendance at Protestant church services compulsory. This was followed by other anti-Catholic acts: it was illegal to bring papal bulls into England, it was high treason to call the queen heretical, it was outlawed to belong to or to reconcile others to the Catholic Church ('persuading to popery'). There was also an Act against Jesuit priests and seminary priests. It was high treason for a priest to be in the queen's dominions and a felony to assist them. A great number of martyrs from 1585 were condemned under this Act.

It was also a difficult time for Elizabeth as queen and leader. There was war with France and Scotland, and the religious Catholic persecution was weakening the queen's authority. There was no Archbishop of Canterbury and nine bishoprics were vacant. Reginald Cardinal Pole, the last Catholic holder of the office of Archbishop of Canterbury, died only a few hours after Queen Mary.

At the time of her accession, Elizabeth had already passed

through some twenty years in which her fortunes had ebbed and flowed, including those under the reign of her sister Mary.

There had to be an immediate religious settlement, as all other state policies would work from it. A supremacy bill went to parliament and was passed at the third attempt. It was very similar to the supremacy as Henry VIII had assumed it. Elizabeth titled herself Supreme Governor, in place of Supreme Head, which would give less offence to her subjects. It allowed her to deprive about two hundred clergymen of their livings and to arbitrate in disputes that were connected with the Church – one example was whether surgeons had the right to prescribe internal medicines.

Another delicate use of the bill was that of uniformity. The Book of Common Prayer followed, to a large extent, the second prayer book of Edward VI. It tried to widen access to Communion for worshippers in parish churches. Words were chosen so that there would be no offence to conscientious Protestants and Catholics. It was compulsory for the clergy to use this prayer book. At the third offence they could be imprisoned for life. The laity was expected to go to church every Sunday. Being absent without reasonable excuse had a fine of one shilling. Rules were drawn up about ceremonies and ornaments, clerical marriage was once again allowed and some former married clergy came back to their posts.

Elizabeth appointed Matthew Parker as Archbishop of Canterbury. He had been chaplain to her mother, Anne Boleyn. Her bishops were worthy men; the Archbishop drafted articles of belief defining the doctrine of the Church and he worked out a new translation of the Bible. England was once again a Protestant country.

Pope Pius V started to combat Protestantism with all his might, wherever it appeared. He was unaware that his power in international politics had fundamentally weakened. He decided to issue a papal bull in 1570, which excommunicated Queen Elizabeth and in theory released her subjects from their allegiance to her. This bull failed, but both Protestants and Catholics right through Elizabeth's reign had a remorseless struggle.

Elizabeth's long reign brought with it expansion of trade, prosperity and flourishing arts. For many in Lancashire, however, it was a time of difficulty and increased persecution. This was particularly true of those in the south-west of the county, very many of whom refused to accept Elizabeth's self-pronounced position as Supreme Governor. In the hundred of West Derby, Lancashire, most people, including almost all gentry and yeomen, remained faithful to the Catholic Church. They were called 'popish recusants'.

The term 'popish recusant' is defined as:

> Convicted for not repairing to some church, chapel or usual place of common prayer to hear divine service there, but forbearing the same, contrary to the tenor of the laws and statutes heretofore made and provided in that behalf.

In 1553, a statute of Edward VI applied this to persons who refused to pay tithes. In 1561, an instance occurs of its use by the ecclesiastical commissioners to denote a group of Catholics who rejected the settlement of religion as established by the Act of Uniformity of 1559.

Later, the term was used for persons who refused to attend the prayer book services of the Church of England prescribed by the Act. Many landed gentry refused to attend their parish church; they encouraged their tenants to follow their example. Acts of Uniformity (1552 and 1559) imposed fines on them to reinforce the establishment of the Church of England; the queen levied a fine of twelve pence for each offence on those who did not attend these services at their parish church, but this seems largely to have been ignored. This was certainly rarely levied in Lancashire, as most of the justices of the peace were either Catholics or Catholic sympathisers themselves, although the vicar of Prescot, Lancashire, in 1604, stated that Catholics were only in the minority.

However, on 2 October 1584, a seminary priest, John Lister, was arrested in Prescot and taken to London with Robert Pilkington of Standish, Lancashire, and committed to the Marshalsea prison, Southwark, on 15 March 1585.

As Elizabeth's reign progressed, she and her advisers had fears and anxieties about those who would not conform. There was a fear that those powerful people who still adhered to the old faith might call for help from the Catholic monarchs of Europe.

Saint John Almond and the Society of his Time

Things became more serious after Pope Pius V's bull, *regnans in excelis*, of 1570, which excommunicated Elizabeth, and still more so when, ten years later, itinerant missionary priests like Campion came secretly across the English Channel to lead a Jesuit mission to win back England to the Catholic faith. There was no immediate hope from Rome for reconciliation.

In 1568, William Allen, an English recusant, founded Douai College to train men to serve as missionaries in England. It was then not long before other colleges were established at Rome and elsewhere. In 1579, Pope Gregory XIII set up a Jesuit college in Rome where John Almond (Ioannes Almondus) would go to train as a missionary priest. A severe training programme was imposed upon the students, who were to be fully trained for martyrdom. They were told to avoid all political controversy and concentrate simply on the conversion of the English people by every possible means. By 1580, there were over a hundred priests at work in England as part of this mission. Their work was constantly made more difficult by attempts from Rome to drag them into political sabotage, even encouraging assassination attempts on Queen Elizabeth on the grounds that whoever did so with pious motives would not be seen as a sinner but would gain merit.

Many of those who took part in the mission to England were members of the Society of Jesus – among them, Edmund Campion and Robert Persons, who came secretly across the English Channel to lead a Jesuit mission to win back England to the Catholic faith. Campion was born in London and was a fellow of St John's College, Oxford. He studied at Douai and was admitted to the Society of Jesus in Rome in 1573. He was ordained as a priest at Prague in 1578 and upon his return to England he worked on the Mission from 1580–1581. He was a noble-hearted and fearless missionary, who quickly made himself popular with and respected by English people. After only a few months of missionary work, he was captured, tortured and hanged, drawn and quartered on 1 December 1581. Persons was very different, an adventurer and lover of intrigue. Because he also worked for a foreign-armed invasion, he offended most of the English Catholics. When he died, he was rector of the college in Rome.

Queen Elizabeth I, 1533-1603

These Catholic missions were considered dangerous by Elizabeth and her government, and they suspected every Catholic as a possible traitor. Because of the possibility of armed rebellion by Catholics, more severe recusancy laws came into place to try and destroy the 'Roman' Catholic Church in England. In 1593, for instance, Gilbert Layton, recusant, confessed to a Jesuit plot to kill Queen Elizabeth. In 1581, it was high treason for a priest to say the Mass. By 1586, recusancy fines were fixed at £20 a month for non-attendance at the parish church services, and a Catholic landowner could lose two-thirds of his land if he persisted in defying the law. One of Elizabeth's greatest ministers, Lord Burghley, drew a rough map showing the seats of the nobility and gentry and marked the names of recusants. The copyright for Lord Burghley's Map of Lancashire is held by the British Museum. Most Lancashire Catholics endured these penalties with remarkable patience. Most Catholics took no part in plots against Elizabeth, but were quietly determined to continue in their faith.

The penal laws against Catholics between 1571 and 1610 were extended but rarely enforced. The government of 1593 sought to introduce sever measures against Catholics such as the removal of children over the age of seven from their homes and the exclusion of Catholics from high office. The method favoured by Tudors for ridding themselves of opponents was to stage an execution without trial, if convenient. The title and possessions of the condemned prisoner would pass to the Crown.

Certain other offences could be deemed acts of recusancy and those convicted of them were labelled a 'popish recusant convict'. The missionaries worked in secret and laws made their activities, under one heading or another, capital offences. The government had its secret service agents, some of them unsavoury types, who often penetrated the missionary priests' secrets. Alice Hogge, in her recent book, entitles them 'God's secret agents'.[45]

In 1585, despite arrests, there were still over twenty Catholic priests active in Lancashire. The war with Spain increased anxiety, with fear of a Spanish landing on the Lancashire coast. In 1590, more Lancashire recusants were imprisoned, others fined, but this

---

[45] Hogge, Alice, *God's Secret Agents*, London, Harper Perennial, 2005

did not reduce the number of Catholics in Lancashire. In England, the number of those who died during the reign of Elizabeth on various charges, particularly for their faith, including those who died in prison, was around two hundred and fifty.

Next in line to the throne after Elizabeth was her cousin, Mary Queen of Scots, a devout Catholic, who considered she was true Queen of England. On the evening of 16 May 1568, a fishing boat came into the harbour at Workington in Cumberland and Mary came ashore. Reaching Carlisle Castle, she planned to throw herself on Elizabeth's mercy after abdicating the Scottish throne in favour of her son James. In fact, Elizabeth kept Mary under house arrest for twenty years in various manor houses. Mary became the focus of Catholic plots to get rid of Elizabeth as queen. Eventually, Mary was taken to Fotheringay Castle in Northamptonshire and charged with treason. Elizabeth refused to sign her cousin's death warrant. She wavered for three months until, in February 1587, she had no choice but to sign the warrant. Mary was executed there a few days later.

In 1588, the defeat of the Armada and other influences converged on the minds of Elizabeth's subjects. Universities were now not just for the education of the clergy, and employment in public service was ceasing to be just for clerics. Laymen then began to have further education at Oxford and Cambridge. But the background was gloomy and religious divisions were becoming irreconcilable. Two new statues in 1593 confirmed the purpose of the government to repress dissent by force. Heavily increased fines for recusants not attending church made almost any Catholic priest liable to the death penalty.

Elizabeth reigned for forty-five years, during which there were only four occasions when persons of exalted rank suffered the penalty of death. She lived into her seventieth year – something no English sovereign had done before. When Elizabeth died on 24 March 1603 there was lamentation and much weeping in the palace in Richmond.

The Venerable English College, Rome

John Almond arrived at the English College as a pilgrim on Palm Sunday, 14 April 1597. He was admitted as a student a fortnight later. John is listed in the college *Liber Ruber* (Red Book) giving details of his arrival and achievements. He signs himself in Latin – Ioannes Almondus:

> IOANNES Almondus Diocesis Cestrensis annos natus xx habens primam Tonsuram aptus ad Phisicam aggrediendam receptus fuit in hoc Anglorum Collegium inter Alumnos Smi D.N. Papae Clementis viii a R.P. Alphonzo Agazzario praedicti Collegii Rectore de expresso mandato Illustrissi mi Carddinalis Burghesii Viceprotectoris Die xiii Aprilis 1597.
>
> Ego praedictus iuro vt supra   Ionnes Almondus
> Accepit 4or minores ordines anno 1597 die 30 nouembris et (illegible erasure) 20 decembris. Et anno 1598 4o Ianuarii et 6 eiusdem anno 1598
> Subdiaconus factus 17 Mar: 1601. Diaconsus 7. Aprilis
> Sacerdos 21 Aprilis eiusdem anni
> Discessit a Collegio Angliam uersus 16 Setemb. Ao Domini 1602. Martyrio glorioso coronatus est mense Non. 1612

This *Liber Ruber* entry translates as follows:

> John Almond of the Diocese of Chester, aged twenty, having his first haircut (tonsura = trimming, shearing), being ready to undertake/tackle physics, was received into the English College among the students/disciples of the most holy DN Pope Clement VIII by the RA Alphonzo Agazzario, director of the aforementioned college, on the express instruction of the most illustrious Cardinal Baronius the Viceprotector on the 14 day of April 1597.

> I, the aforementioned sear ... the above.   John Almond
> He received the four minor orders ... in the year 1597 on the 30 day of November and ... on the 4 day of January and the 6 day of the same month in the year 1598.
>
> He was made subdeacon on the 17 March 1601, deacon 7 April and priest the 21 April in the same year. He left the college for England on about 16 September in the year of our Lord, 1602. He was crowned with glorious martyrdom in the month November 1612.

As we see in the *Liber Ruber* entry, John received the four minor orders during the first year at the college, and within twelve months he was conducting a scholastic disputation in philosophy. To judge from the college expense accounts this was an elaborate affair: his arguments were printed and covered three-hundred sheets, and there was a banquet to round off the occasion. Three years later, in 1601, he was ordained priest in Rome, and in the following year he completed his study of theology. To gain his DD – 'Doctor of Divinity' – he 'publicly sustained theses of universal divinity with great applause'[46] at the Roman College, later to become the Gregorian University. This disputation was, if anything, even more magnificent than the earlier one and John Almond acquitted himself with great distinction. Cardinal Baronius, to whom he dedicated his written theses, was quite overcome, embracing him and kissing his tonsure. There was music and bell-ringers were employed. As one life remarks, 'a foreshadowing, this, of a more spectacular defence he would have to conduct under an English gallows.' Indeed, the next time he appeared in public theological debate he was on trial for his life in England.

The college has been known as the Venerable English College since 1818 because of the forty-four students who were martyred for the Catholic faith between 1581 and 1679, as well as the 130 who suffered imprisonment and exile. Forty-one of these have been canonised or beatified by the Church:

---

[46] Steele, *Blessed John Almond*, p.4

1581	St Ralph Sherwin	1594	Blessed George Haydock
1582	St Luke Kirby	1594	Blessed Edward Thwing
1582	Blessed John Shert	1595	St Robert Southwell SJ
1582	Blessed Thomas Cottam	1595	St Henry Walpole SJ
1582	Blessed William Lacey	1601	Blessed Robert Middleton
1583	Blessed William Hart	1602	Blessed Robert Watkinson
1584	Blessed Thomas Hemerford	1602	Venerable Thomas Tichborne
1584	Blessed John Munden	1606	Blessed John Oldcorne
1586	Blessed John Lowe	1612	Blessed Richard Smith
1588	Blessed Robert Morton	**1612**	**St John Almond**
1588	Blessed Richard Leigh	1616	Blessed John Thules
1588	Blessed Edward James	1642	Blessed John Lockwood
1588	Blessed Christopher Buxton	1642	Venerable Edward Morgan
1590	Blessed Christopher Bales	1643	Venerable Brian Tansfield SJ
1590	Blessed Edmund Duke	1645	St Henry More SJ
1591	St Polydore Plasden	1646	Blessed John Woodcock OFM
1591	St Eustace White	1678	Venerable Edward Mico SJ
1592	Blessed Joseph Lambton	1679	St David Lewis SJ
1592	Blessed Thomas Portmort	1679	Blessed Anthony Turner SJ
1594	Blessed John Cornelius, SJ	1679	St John Wall OFM
1594	Blessed John Ingram		

The seminary was for English candidates for the Catholic priesthood. It was founded in 1362 as a hospice for English pilgrims. In 1578, Pope Gregory XIII converted it into a seminary for training missionaries for England. Students had to take an oath to go to England when it should seem good to their superiors. Soon afterwards its direction was entrusted to the Jesuits, who were in charge of it until the suppression of the society in 1773. It then passed into the hands of Italian secular priests (all clergy who did not belong to the rule of a religious order), under whose direction it remained until it was closed during the invasion of the French. In 1818, Pope Pius VII restored it, and since then its rectors have always been members of the English secular clergy. The college is still used today.

Several of John Almond's contemporaries at the English College died for their faith:

BLESSED RICHARD NEWPORT (ALIAS SMITH) – was in Newgate with John. He was a seminary priest, born at Ashby St Legers, Northants. Ordained in 1599, he worked on the English mission in the London district. He was condemned for priesthood and was hanged, drawn and quartered at Tyburn 30 May 1612.

BLESSED JOHN LOCKWOOD (ALIAS LASCELLES) – must have been known by John. He was a seminary priest, born at Sowerby, North Riding, Yorkshire. Ordained in 1597, on the English mission 1598–1642. He was condemned for priesthood, then hanged, drawn and quartered at York, 13 April 1642.

BLESSED ROBERT WATKINSON was a seminary priest, born in Hemingbrough, East Riding, Yorkshire and educated at Hemingbrough and Castleford then Douai. He was ordained in March 1602. Later he was condemned for priesthood, and was then hanged, drawn and quartered (aged 23) at Tyburn on 20 April 1602. William Alabaster, the apostate, was also with him for a while.

BLESSED ROBERT MIDDLETON OF YORK. A seminary priest and later a Jesuit, he must have been impressed by the Jesuit rule when at Rome. This was a religious order founded by the Spaniard Ignatius Loyola in 1534, specifically to quash heresy. Pope Paul III recognised the order in 1540 and henceforth its activities were directed by the papacy. Soon after Robert arrived back in England he applied for admission into the Society of Jesus. However, he was arrested almost at once and although Father Henry Garnet, the English Superior, wrote to tell him his desire had been granted, he could not be certain the message was received. Robert had studied at Douai and then Rome where he was ordained as a priest in 1585. He worked on the mission in Lancashire, Yorkshire and Cheshire for fifteen years. He was condemned for priesthood, then hanged, drawn and quartered at Lancaster on or around 3 April 1601.

A student at the college in those years would hardly be bored. The mettlesome Elizabethan students were young men of their time, and were often in conflict with authority. A group of malcontents had been giving trouble just before John Almond arrived. There had been deputations to the Pope, marches and counter-marches. Shortly after John's arrival, a number of these young bloods had been found carousing in a tavern. An attempt to pass themselves off as Germans failed, and one of them was sent to prison. (It is said, with what foundation we know not, that the conspicuous red cassock worn today by students of the German College originates from this affair.)

After the ringleaders had left for Douai and the new rector, Father Robert Persons (the famous Jesuit who had accompanied Campion to England and founded the seminaries at Valladolid and Seville) had introduced a regime of much-needed strictness, peace descended. This independent spirit was disciplined and channelled so that it could be used where it was most needed – in an England where every inducement was offered to follow the crowd and conform. The only disturbance after Persons' installation came from without. From 1598, the tragedy of the archpriest controversy was to disrupt English Catholic life, setting the clergy at variance each other over the question of Church government. Its effects were soon felt in Rome: Persons took a leading part when the case was brought to the Holy See, and on the Pope's orders two of the appellant[47] secular priests were kept in custody at the college. One doubts if the students were permitted to have anything to do with the priests, but John Almond must have seen them and probably spoke to them on occasions.

John Almond left for England in September 1602, while the controversy was at its height, to enter a country where Catholics were no longer untried as earlier, in a common struggle, but sadly and suicidally divided. He was in the company with John Copley, who had just been ordained and was later to apostatise and marry. They arrived at Douai in October, where the Douai Diaries report that 'they rested after their journey and purchased the necessary clothes. In just over a fortnight they left for England'[48]. The 'necessary clothes' would of course be lay dress. In what guise and by what route John Almond reached England we do not know, nor what contacts he made on arrival. All too many seminary priests were captured as soon as they stepped off the boat, so efficient was Elizabeth's security system and so poorly organised were the Catholics. John must have been thankful that he had at least arrived unobserved.

---

[47] 'Appellant' was the name given to those secular priests who opposed the appointment of the archpriest Blackwell. Thirty-one secular priests, led by William Bishop, appealed to Rome to cancel the appointment of George Blackwell as archpriest and superior of the English mission on the grounds that the pro-Jesuit policy was harming the Catholic cause in England. This initial appeal was unsuccessful but further appeals in 1601 and 1602, with the backing of the French ambassador, resulted in Blackwell's reprimand and, in January 1603, a renunciation of the policy to replace Queen Elizabeth. Father John Mush, one of the appellants who had been Margaret Clitherow's confessor and her biographer, 'commanded the scholars not to speak to any of us' (Steele, *Blessed John Almond*, p.5). The two appellants kept in custody by Father Persons were William Bishop and Robert Cannock.
[48] Steele, *Blessed John Almond*, p.6

King James I of England

The question of Elizabeth's successor was a delicate one. Elizabeth had no children, but her subjects were relieved when she named James VI of Scotland, a Protestant king, as heir – the son of Mary Queen of Scots. There was a feeling of relief that the succession had been settled at last and, further, that James was a staunch Protestant. James VI of Scotland became James I of England in 1603, shortly after John Almond had returned as a missionary priest to England.

The first parliament of James looked at religious questions and at first seemed to be strongly sympathetic with the Puritans and hostile to the Catholics. It was James' intention to promote peace and unity in religious matters, but few people understood his thinking on the matter. As a theologian, he made a serious study of the intellectual issues on which the country was divided. He had been in touch with continental Catholics before his accession and this had raised hope that he would interpret the existing church settlement favourably for the recusants. The statutory fines were not enforced by him. He hoped that the pope would cooperate with him to make the distinction between Catholicism and treason clear by authorising the excommunication of extremists. This was not accepted and he felt he could take no further action. His leniency towards the Catholics ended and he took measures to banish priests and levy the full fines on the richer recusants.

James was the great grandson of Margaret Tudor, sister of Henry VIII. In her first marriage to King James IV of Scotland, she had a son, James V. During her second marriage to the Earl of Angus she had a daughter, Lady Margaret Douglas, who married the Earl of Lennox. James V's only legitimate child was Mary Queen of Scots and the Earl and Countess of Lennox had a son,

Saint John Almond and the Society of his Time

Henry Lord Darnley. The marriage of Mary Queen of Scots and Darnley – who both stood in line for the throne of England – produced a son, James. He became King of Scotland in 1567 when he was only one year old, and he inherited his parents' joint claim to the throne of England in 1603 – this then was the union of the English and Scottish crowns, but James never forgot he was King of Scotland.

His English subjects, on the whole, made him welcome and titles of honour were scattered around. He brought some Scots with him to the English court and some of them became objects of jealousy with the English nobility. His personal qualities were not popular with the English aristocracy. He was a theologian, author and an indiscreet talker, with a good sense of humour. His policy was to keep the country as he found it, but to reconcile its differences.

James only had four parliaments. The first, in 1604, lasted for four sessions spread over six years. He never succeeded in working harmoniously with the Commons. Objections were ignored by the 'high and mighty' James. He believed that God had ordained kings to rule – the Divine Right of Kings. He ruled without a parliament from 1614–1621.

When parliament was about to meet for its second session in the autumn of 1605, a small group of Catholic hotheads stuffed a cellar under the House of Lords with gunpowder. Parliament then passed a new law against recusants and made sure that the country would remember the Gunpowder Plot. Special prayers were added to the Prayer Book. This anniversary was kept thus until 1859. It is still kept today in the form of Bonfire Night.

If Catholics were deceived in their hopes of relief, the Puritans were equally disappointed. They too expected a relaxation of restrictions and presented a petition, called the Millenary Petition. It claimed to represent the views of a thousand clergy. It mentioned the inactivity of the parochial clergy and the holdings of livings by non-residents. James agreed with the Puritans that the Prayer Book needed some revision. The Puritans hoped for concessions on confirmation rites, the use of vestments, ceremonies and the Articles of Belief. They suggested a conference on these matters. The bishops did not agree, but were overruled by

King James I of England

the king, who granted the Puritans' request. This council met in January 1604. Slight changes were made to the Prayer Book and some matters concerning ecclesiastical courts. This was dealt with by committees made up of bishops alone and bishops with members of the Privy Council. The reform was whittled down in their hands to almost nothing. One result of the conference was the commissioning of the authorised (King James) version of the Bible, one of the cornerstones of the English language, which was completed in 1611. This had an enduring impact wherever the English language and the Anglican Church spread.

James became unpopular with the Puritans, angering them by refusing to pass the religious reforms they wanted. A steadily increasing company broke away from the Anglican Church and formed non-conformist groups. In the south-east of Lancashire, most non-conformists were Presbyterians.

James was extravagant, especially in the gifts he gave to his male favourites, and at one time he was forced to borrow money from his wife's goldsmith. His passions were theology, the hunt and handsome young men, for it is believed he may have been homosexual. Although he was very intelligent, he liked nothing more than the sound of his own voice and earned himself the nickname 'the wisest fool in Christendom'. He was said to be a very messy eater and to have a bad temper.

John Almond's Later Life

THE MISSIONARY PRIEST, 1602–1612

Not much is known of the work that John did as a missionary, but this is not surprising – publicity was not something he wanted. However, there are occasional references to his pastoral work in letters and records, and all of these suggest that most of his work took place in and around London. A letter that John wrote in 1604 to his former rector, Father Persons, enquiring about his brother, places him in the capital in that year:

> Reverend Father,
>
> This bearer upon other occasion of business being resolved to travel so far as the place where you remain, thought also to defer his resolution in matters of religion until he came thither. But being touched afterwards with the uncertainty of his arrival, and certain danger of his soul, if death should have prevented his designment, he altered his resolution and is become Catholic ... it pleased God to make me the instrument of his reconciliation. Your charity I know will show him that favour and kind entertainment which usually you do to strangers of his quality and condition; but something more (much I dare not desire because my deserts are few or none) I hope he shall find at my request, and I shall not fail to remain thankful.
>
> Concerning my brother I ... can hear no certainty whether he be in Spain or Italy, religious or as before; no, not so much as whether he be dead or living. I heard he was bitten by a mad dog in his return from Compostella, but as yet I cannot learn any more. Good Father, let me humbly request you to certify me concerning him as soon as you can possibly find the means. I

> remain about London, Mr Blunt well knoweth the place of my abode.
>
> Thus humbly recommending myself to your Reverence, with great desire to be made partaker in the prayers of that virtuous company, I leave to trouble you any further.
>
> London, this 16th of April, AD 1604
> Your assured and dutiful child,
> John Almond[49]

The discretion needed at this time is clear from the absence of the name of the bearer, the recipient and Almond's address. Although he signs himself by his real name, this was not the one by which he was known (as previously mentioned he was known by two aliases: Francis Lathome or [Latham] and Molyneux). It is possible that the bearer was Anthony Timcock, a solicitor's clerk reconciled to the Church by Father Almond. He travelled to Rome shortly after his conversion and entered the English College at Valladolid. It has also been suggested that his brother, Henry, was a priest. If the bearer was Anthony Timcock, it is fair to assume that John Almond was in contact with lawyers at this time. The lawyers' quarter of London was in Holborn – the location of his arrest in 1607. Therefore, it is possible that from 1604 onwards John concentrated his efforts on this area of London.

The lawyers' quarters could have been Staple Inn whose Elizabethan façade still stands in Holborn, opposite Grays Inn Road. The inn dates back to the reign of Elizabeth I in 1580. It was one of the inns of Chancery that were established to assist young men in learning the original and something of the elements of the law before they moved on to one of the greater Inns of Court.

In *Memoirs of Missionary Priests*, Bishop Challoner discusses Almond's appearance and character during his years of apostolic work. This contemporary sketch is helpful in bringing about an image of Almond at this time. He says:

> I have met with little or nothing of the particulars of his missionary labours, only my author (the manuscript) gives him

---

[49] Steele, *Blessed John Almond*, p.6

the following character, in his introduction to the account of his death: ... 'a man of forty-five, by his own relation; yet in his countenance more grave and staid, beginning to be besprinkled with hairs that were white – who having tarried beyond the seas about ten years to enable himself by his study with learning and virtue, returned into his native country, where he exercised an holy life with all sincerity, and a singular good content to those that knew him, and worthily deserved both a good opinion of his learning and sanctity of life; a reprover of sin, a good example to follow; of an ingenious and acute understanding, sharp and apprehensive in his conceits and answers, yet complete with modesty, full of courage, and ready to suffer for Christ, that suffered for him. Of his stature, neither high nor low, but indifferent; a body lean, either by nature or through ghostly discipline; a face lean, his head blackish brown; in his conversation mild, learned and persuasive, and worthy to be remembered of those that did converse with him. As I said, not only a sharp reprover of sin, but a good encourager besides, by his own example, of those that sought the way to heaven, which he himself found at the last by persecutions, crosses, and many afflictions.' So far the manuscript.[50]

First Arrest – 1607

John did not last long in Holborn. Indeed, three years after his letter to Father Persons he was tracked to a house by determined pursuivants, who broke in and arrested him. The following Italian report, kept in the Jesuit archives in Rome, describes the moment of the arrest:

> The great success of his apostolate spread abroad, and soon reached the ears of the King's Ministers. Fuelled with rage and gated they fell upon the saintly priest. With the rough pursuivants at his back he was taken away a prisoner, cast into a pitch-black gaol called Newgate and loaded with chains.[51]

Newgate, the chief criminal prison, was first used as a prison in the early Middle Ages. The prison contained a great store of

---

[50] From: Challoner, *Memoirs of Missionary Priests*, p.330
[51] Steele, *Blessed John Almond*, p.7

John Almond's Later Life

priests and other Catholics, to whom people of all sorts had continual access. It was burned down during anti-Catholic riots in 1780. John was later moved from Newgate to the Gatehouse Prison in Westminster, where it is likely that he was a fellow prisoner of Father Thomas Garnet SJ, one of the Forty Martyrs and the nephew of Father Henry Garnet SJ, who was executed for his alleged involvement in the Gunpowder Plot. The Gatehouse prison was noted for its sheer corruption. Recusants were able to bribe their jailers to pass letters to their friends to tell them what they had been asked when examined and they then got back vital information which enabled them to guess shrewdly how to answer. Unfortunately the comparatively free conditions at the Gatehouse could also be used by the government for its own purposes.

Shortly after John's capture he escaped or was released. In 1609 he was in Staffordshire, where he signed a petition for a bishop to be appointed for English Catholics. Unfortunately this is all that is known of his pastoral work.

In 1612 he was captured again and brought for questioning. The details of this capture are more fully documented. He was questioned before a Justice of the Peace and Dr King, Bishop of London. A report of his interrogation, attributed to the hand of Almond himself and quoted by William J Steele reads as follows:

The Bishop:	What is your name?
John Almond:	My name is Francis.
The Bishop:	What else?
John Almond:	Lathome.
The Bishop:	Is your name not Molineux?
John Almond:	No.
The Bishop:	I think it shall prove it to be so.
John Almond:	You will have more to do, than you ever had to do in your life.
The Bishop:	What countryman are you?
John Almond:	A Lancashire man.

The Bishop:	In what place were you born?
John Almond:	About Allerton.
The Bishop:	About Allerton! mark the equivocation; then, not in Allerton?
John Almond:	No equivocation; I was not born in Allerton, but in the edge or side of Allerton.
The Bishop:	You were born under a hedge, then, were you?
John Almond:	Many a better man than I, or you either, has been born under a hedge.
The Bishop:	What, you cannot remember that you were born in a house?
John Almond:	Can you?
The Bishop:	My mother told me so.
John Almond:	Then you remember not that you were born in a house, but only that Your mother told you so; so much I remember too.
The Bishop:	Were you ever beyond the seas?
John Almond:	I have been in Ireland.
The Bishop:	How long since you came thence?
John Almond:	I remember not how long since, neither is it material.
The Bishop:	Here is plain answering, is it not?
John Almond:	More plain than you would give, if you were examined yourself before some of ours in another place.
The Bishop:	I ask, are you a priest?
John Almond:	I am not Christ; and unless I was Christ, in your own grounds, yours I mean, I cannot be a priest.
The Bishop:	Though you cannot be one in our grounds, are you one in your own?
John Almond:	If I be none, nor can be any in your grounds, which allow no other Priesthood, nor other

John Almond's Later Life

>priest but Christ, and you are bound to maintain your own grounds, and uphold the truth of them, you might well forbear this question, and suppose for certain that I am no priest.

The Bishop: Are you a priest, yea or no?

John Almond: No man accuseth me,

The Bishop: Then, this is all the answer I shall have?

John Almond: All I can give unless proof come in.

The Bishop: Where have you lived, and in what have you spent your time?

John Almond: Here is an orderly course of justice, sure! What is it material where I Lived, or how I have spent my time, all the while I am accused of no evil?

The Bishop: Will you take the oath of allegiance?

John Almond: Any oath of allegiance, if it contain nothing but allegiance.

(And with that the Bishop reaches out his arm for the oath, lying towards the middle of the table; which I perceiving said —)

>That oath you cannot with a good conscience offer.

The Bishop: Yes, that I can; and I thank God, I have taken it myself seven times.

John Almond: God forbid!

The Bishop: Why?

John Almond: You have been seven times perjured.

The Bishop: Wherein?

John Almond: In taking this false clause 'and I do further swear that I do from my heart abhor, detest, and abjure as impious and heretical, this damnable doctrine and position, that princes excommunicated or deprived by the Pope may be deposed, etc.

The Bishop: There is no perjury nor falsehood in it.

John Almond: If in taking it you abjure that position as heretical which is not heretical then it is perjury and falsehood to take it. But in taking it you abjure that position as heretical which is not heretical, ergo, etc.

The Bishop: I grant your major, I deny your minor.

John Almond: No position in your grounds can be heretical, unless it be expressly censured for heretical, by the word of God, or the contradictory expressly contained in the word of God. But this position is not expressly censured for heretical by the word of God; nor is the contradictory expressed in the word of God. Ergo, it is not heretical.

The Bishop: It is censured as heretical by the word.

John Almond: Allege the text, give us a bible.

The Bishop: Bring in a bible.

(Then turning to it with an evil will, he said it was censured in the 13th of the Romans.)

John Almond: You mean those words, He that resisteth power, resisteth God's ordinance. But I ask, where is this position censured? There is not a one word of the position in hand.

(Other place he alleged none.)

The Bishop: You would have it censured in express words?

John Almond: You are bound to bring a censure in express words: which, because I see you cannot, answer this consequence: 'This position is not set down at all in the bible: ergo it cannot be censured by the bible.'

(He answered not; but said, I was a proud arrogant Jack. To which I replied, 'God forgive you, your words trouble me not'; and so two several times more I prayed God to forgive him, when he miscalled me and abused me in words.)[52]

---

[52] Steele, *Blessed John Almond*, pp.8–10

John Almond's Later Life

In *Memoirs of Missionary Priests*, the account is also quoted and continues from this point as follows:

> Then leaving the oath, which he was weary of, he asked, Have you gone to any church? And added, I forgot it before; but I go beyond you now. A. I have not gone to the church. B. Will you go? A. I will not: Is not this plain dealing? B. Now you deal plainly. A. If it would not offend you, I must tell you that you went beyond youself: for you confessed even now that you should have asked it before, and so go beyond yourself in asking it now. Much more passed betwixt us before about a disjunctive position, wherein the Bishop needeth not to boast of his logic; at part of which a certain Dean coming in, after the Bishop was weary the Dean began to talk of the Pope's power to depose kings, saying, It was essential to the Pope, and a matter of faith in our doctrine, To whom I replied, It was not essential to the Pope's power, nor any matter of faith; and that, whether the Pope could or could not depose, it was perjury to take the oath in their grounds, and ours too; which, I said, I would undertake to demonstrate before all the bishops in England, or else I would lose my hand and my head. The Dean said, I was too quick with him; and that my logic would deceive me, if I builded so much upon it; wishing me to look to a good conscience. I replied, It was my conscience, which I did stand upon, and therefore refused the oath for the reasons alleged. Yet to give satisfaction, this oath I offered that I would swear. I do bear in my heart and soul so much allegiance to King James (whom I prayed God to bless now and evermore) as he, or any Christian king could expect by the law of nature, the law of God, or the positive law of the true Church, be it which it will, ours or yours. The Bishop and the Dean said they were fair words; but the Dean added, he knew well which Church I meant; to which I answered, Let you and me try that, and then put it out of the question; but he was deaf on that ear.
>
> Then the Bishop bade me put my hand to my examination. I first perused it; and in the end of it, where the register had set down, Being asked whether he would take the oath of allegiance, he answered, He could not without perjury; I bid him add also, as I had said, I could not in their grounds or ours; the Bishop would not suffer him to add that, but said I should have another time; upon that, I put my hand to it, though I said he had put it in by halves. Thus ended the pageant, saving that I said publicly (giving

> the honour to God) that I had not sworn any oath, not so much as in faith, in sixteen years before; and therefore they neede not wonder that I now refused an oath with falsehood and perjury in it.[53]

After Almond's examination, an indictment was brought against him under the *Statute 27 Elizabeth*, which made it treason for an English subject to be ordained by Roman authority and remain in England. It was then that he was taken to Newgate where he had to await his trial.

TIME IN JAIL

The jailor at Newgate, a man called Price, treated the Catholic prisoners very badly. He was not reprimanded for this – indeed, he had the support of the authorities who were still reeling from the Gunpowder Plot. The influence of the bishops under James I was also growing, and some writers have suggested that the Archbishop of Canterbury 'was personally responsible for the inhuman treatment of the Catholic prisoners'[54]. The prisoners were unable to rest and the foul smells in the dungeon were so bad that they left them in danger of suffocating.

There was certainly a lot of animosity between Almond and Price. In one letter, Steele tells us, 'John calls Price his "enemy", and imputes to him the fact that he was brought to trial and sentenced'[55]. A full letter written by Father Henry Cooper, one of John's fellow prisoners, describes the treatment they received:

> 'Good sir – I am sure you have heard of the inhuman dealing of our new keeper with us, putting us all into Justice Hall without commodity of lodging; forcing divers of us to sit up night by night, and yet exacting money for beds, debarring all access of friends, suffering the pursuivants to seize such as come unto our gate, yea, vexing even Protestants themselves that come unto us. Neither can we have any remedy against him, such is the malice of the Bishop, who maintaineth all injuries done unto us. Our

---

[53] From: Challoner, *Memoirs of Missionary Priests,* pp.332–333
[54] Steele, *Blessed John Almond*, p.11
[55] Ibid.

John Almond's Later Life

keeper's pride is in that excess, as overruled with passion he will admit of no reason, insomuch as we are wholly ignorant of what course to take whereby we may best redeem our vexations. Our comfort only is, that the cause for which we suffer is good and honourable, being for God Himself; and these our miseries are infallible signs of His love towards us, according to that of the Apostle: 'Quem diligit Dominus castigat, flagellat autem omnem filium quem recipit' ... ('For whom the Lord loveth he chastiseth; and he scourgeth every son whom he receiveth' – Heb. XII, 6.)

'In the meantime I would desire your good prayers for us, that we may so endure these our troubles, as they may turn to God's greater honour and glory, and our souls' comfort ... I humbly take my leave on this 10th November, 1612, though never leave to be

Yours,

HEN. COOPER[56]

There are other reasons for Price being so awful to the prisoners, all of which revolve around the politics of the time. One prominent reason is the sermon that the Archbishop of Canterbury gave at the Prince of Wales's funeral. It was during this sermon that he implied that the prince's death was a punishment from God for having too lenient a policy towards the papists. However, it was not only Price that John Almond had to contend with while in jail. He also disputed with Protestant ministers including George Abbot (then the Archbishop of Canterbury) and Bishop King. Steele sees this in a positive light, saying it was 'a rare compliment, surely, and a clear indication of his importance in their eyes. A recantation from this holy and well-regarded priest would have the greatest value'[57]. He goes on to quote from Father Grene's account of John Almond, *De Joanne Almondo Martyre*, which tells us that the ministers were disappointed:

> In time of his imprisonment he frequently had conference with the said Archbishop and disputations, and who remaining always overcome was the more cruel in causing him to have bad usage

---
[56] Ibid.
[57] Ibid., p.12

and ... the Arch-minister of London, routed in argument, uttered nothing but threats and warnings. The martyr promptly retorted that he had Christ's word for it that he need not fear those that kill the body, and afterwards can do no more.[58]

John Almond's time in jail was not as time in jail is today. In those days, prisons were places for people to be detained after trial, but places for people to be kept while they waited for a trial. As a result, inmates could linger for years in Newgate, perhaps even dying before their trial date was set. In the London Sessions files, there are lists of 'Catholics in Newgate' whose names never appear on the Newgate calendar for trial or in the records of the trials. If a Catholic was finally brought to court, it was normally only for a special reason or in a special case, as is the case with John Almond.

It is perhaps not surprising that many prisoners tried to escape from these awful conditions, including some twenty or so who made it out while Almond was imprisoned there. However, fear of Price and the retribution if caught was enough to stop John from joining them. Among those who stayed with John were George Fisher and Richard Cooper. As the jailers were unable to punish the escaped inmates, they took their frustration out on the remaining prisoners, perhaps feeling that they may have had a hand in the escape. John Almond explains the realities of this punishment in a letter:

> The Keeper of Newgate has been somewhat hard unto me and others that way, whom God forgive, for I do. For I have been prisoner there since March, we have been ill-treated continually, but now at last without charity; for we were all put down into the hole or dungeon, or place of 'little ease', whence was removed since we came thither two or three cartloads of filth and dirt; we were kept twenty-four hours without bread, or meat or drink, loaded with irons lodging on the damp ground, and so continued for ten days or thereabouts.[59]

---

[58] Ibid.
[59] Ibid., p.13

Most sources tell us that the remaining prisoners were thrown into an area of Newgate known as 'Limbo' where they were starved and given very little water. This area could also have been the infamous 'Little Ease' in the Tower of London. It seems that after John was executed, things got worse for the remaining prisoners:

> After Almond's death, the priests in Newgate were together in an underground dungeon, weighed down with iron fetters, with no light save that of a lantern. Whoever came to the grill to speak to them was seized – even the heretics.[60]

It is amazing then that in these awful conditions the men still managed to stay true to their faith: ' "Yet," says another version, "they ceased not to sing their Office together, in token of thanksgiving to God." '[61]

THE TRIAL

John's fears that he may languish indefinitely in Newgate were quashed when, on Thursday, 3 December 1612 he was taken to trial. This was an extremely sudden development, as Father Robert Jones comments:

> ...when I had finished my letter, a certain learned and venerable priest, named John Almond, formerly a scholar of the English College at Rome, has been suddenly delivered up to judgement.[62]

There are many possible reasons for this sudden and unexpected development. The authorities had become more severe, especially the Ecclesiastics who tried to persuade King James to be so. The new Archbishop of Canterbury, George Abbot, was more severe than his predecessor and there was increased fear of Catholics since the Gunpowder Plot – they were seen as a threat to lives of the king and Parliament. However, it was the escape of John's

---

[60] Ibid.
[61] Ibid.
[62] Ibid.

fellow prisoners that probably influenced his trial date the most, and it is highly likely that the authorities chose such an outstanding priest to try in the hope that it would dissuade the others from misbehaving.

Although the public were wary of Catholic priests because of the way that they had been portrayed since the Gunpowder Plot – as sinister and scheming – this was not always enough to convince a jury to convict, particularly if the individual was as saintly and honourable as John. It is not surprising, perhaps, that it was at this time that Price, the jailor, came forward with an altogether more serious accusation:

> His (John Almond's) enemy Mr Price, keeper of Newgate, did depose against him that he heard him say that he had power to absolve one, though he should kill the king. But Mr Almond upon his oath denied this, and said that he only had said 'through true penitence Ravaillac might be saved. [Francois Ravaillac, a religious fanatic, assassinated Henry IV of France on 16 May, 1610. Executed 27 May, 1610][63]

The stigma attached to an accusation of regicide was undeniably a factor in John's trial. Steele tells us, 'Prices's accusation was invaluable; so much so that there was no attempt to prove Almond's priesthood, let alone any real treason. Propaganda had done its work well'[64]. John was brought to trial at the present-day Old Bailey, then known as the London Sessions House or Justice Hall. There are several accounts of John's trial. One letter reporting it says:

> The third day of December being Thursday, Mr Mollinax alias Ladome alias Almond a Roman priest was carried to the Sessions House, arraigned for a priest, without any man that could witness against him, or accuse him of ought to the great dislike even of Protestants themselves, by reason of such unjust proceeding. He refused to put himself to the verdict of the 12 because there was no proof at all, nor any just suspicion that might be sufficient to condemn him, and therefore he said he was lothe 12 men should

---

[63] Ibid., p.14
[64] Ibid.

John Almond's Later Life

> be guilty of his death, adding moreover that he might be a Frenchman, an Italian or Spaniard, and no Englishman for ought they knew...[65]

Another record, in the form of a manuscript, notes the following details regarding the legal procedure:

> The law lays down that those who refuse to submit their case to a jury shall be 'executed with greater cruelty'. The penalty for refusing to submit to a jury was pressing to death as happened to Margaret Clitherow of York in 1586. Almond ... chose rather to expose himself to a more painful death ... He did not have his way, however; for the justices, who to find favour with the King and his so-called Archbishop of Canterbury had not scrupled to press him to submit to a jury a case without witness or proof, had no scruples about proceeding with a fresh act of injustice, and contrary to English law, they looked no further for evidence or proof of his priesthood but, as if the matter were proved, established and admitted, they passed judgement on him as being a priest and as having by his priesthood incurred the penalties due to those guilty of high treason; and so for being a priest they sentenced him as a traitor to King and country, to be hanged, drawn and quartered alive, ordering that his bowels should be burned and his head should be set up on London Bridge and his quarters over the city gates to be eaten by the birds.[66]

As soon as John's trial was over, he was taken back to the dungeon where he was greeted by his fellow prisoners and friends. He was kept in the dungeon for one more day and was then led to Tyburn. Tyburn, that place of execution in west London, is recalled today by a stone in the centre of the traffic island at the point where Oxford Street becomes Bayswater Road, a short distance from Marble Arch underground station. Catholics and Protestants alike perished here, in public view, during the time of Queen Mary and Queen Elizabeth I. As twenty-first-century vehicles career around the site today the visitor will have difficulty in conjuring up any sense of horror, public glee and ghoulishness which must have confronted John Almond and other martyrs as

---

[65] Ibid.
[66] Ibid., pp.14–15

they were led to the scaffold – the triangular Tyburn Tree – some eleven feet high, capable of dispatching eight victims at a time and surviving down to the eighteenth century.

At the time of John's expected martyrdom the authorities feared a great crowd of people at the execution, so they spread the rumour that it would not take place until Monday; in fact, it had been arranged for a very early hour on Saturday. Nevertheless, there was a great crowd at Tyburn, waiting for the martyr.

THE MARTYRDOM OF JOHN ALMOND

There are several reports of John Almond's martyrdom, all of which differ slightly but have the same core details. This is the extensive account given in a manuscript which is now kept at Stonyhurst College:

> Being come down to Tyburn and raised up into a cart right underneath the gallows, with a cheerful countenance signing himself with the sign of the Cross, and saying 'In nomine Patris, etc.,' he desired the Sheriff to give him leave to speak, protesting he would not speak any word either against his Majesty or against the State. This the Sheriff did yield unto, but first he would have had him put of his clothes, and speak in his shirt, which he was unwilling to do, urging that he could not speak so well with his clothes off, desiring he might have them on and he would be very brief; which at length was granted him...
>
> He said he was born in Lancashire, the town's name was South Allerton, where he was brought up until he was about eight years old, at which time he was carried over into Ireland, where he remained until he was at man's estate. And when he was last taken, which was on the 22nd of May a year since, no man knew whether he was an Englishman or no. He then being carried before a Justice of the Peace, 'which here,' he said, 'he would not name, to avoid offence,' was by him examined whether he was a priest or no. He did not confess to him that he was. Whereupon the Justice offered him the oath (which he called of allegiance), which by him was refused, in respect that in conscience it could not be taken without danger of perjury, both to his Majesty and to him that shall take it.
>
> Then he, kneeling on his knees, said he took God to witness,

and as he hoped to be saved ... that this which he spake, he spake from his heart, without any manner of dissimulation, that his Majesty was sole and lawful King of this realm, and that he bare so true and loyal a mind to him, as either the King of Spain, or King of France, or any other Catholic prince whatever could desire, either by the laws of God, nature, or nations, of their subjects. He protested also that never in his lifetime any jot or least thought of treason did enter his heart ... and if he should have heard of any intended against his Majesty, he would have revealed it by all means possible.

Then a preacher standing by did ask him whether he held the King to have sufficient power to make laws or no. Before he could answer him, another preacher asked him another question. What it was I know not, but by his answer it seemed to belong to the former question, for he desired him to hold him excused, till he had answered the first, and then he would speak to him.

Then turning to the former he answered his question thus: that the King has sufficient power to make laws in England, as the King of France ... or any other prince ... had to make laws in their own realms. 'But as the King of Spain, France, and all other princes have power to make laws over their own subjects, so likewise both the Kings of England, Spain, France, and all other princes whatsoever are subject to our Saviour Christ Jesus. And ... the kings and other princess ... have no power to make any one law against the law of God, which I hope you will not deny,' speaking to him that first moved the question.

Then turning to the second he answered him in this manner: 'Thus out of St Matthew he proved that our Saviour having power, gave it to His disciples ... and so consecrated priests have it from Him and at His commandment do go through the world to preach the Gospel. This being the law and commandment of the Pope, who is the substitute of Almighty God, to go and preach throughout the world, the priests in England are no traitors in coming to England to preach the faith.'

The first preacher told him he was not executed as a traitor, but as a heretic. But he said again, 'Why was he hanged then and not burned, which is the death of a heretic?' The minister hereupon was silent, and then he went on with his speech as afore.

He told them that he was brought from the Justice of Peace that first examined him and committed to Newgate, where he remained until about ten days since, when seven of the prisoners made an escape out of prison, at which time on Sunday morning he was taken out of his chamber with all the rest that remained, put into a dungeon, filthy and loathsome. The Sheriff said that he did malign the State therein; whereupon he said, 'Good Mr Sheriff, I do not and will not. For I thought that was done by the keeper, and not by the State.' Then going on with his speech, that being cast into that loathsome dungeon where he had scarce meat and drink to sustain nature ... he there was kept till the time that he was brought forth to his arraignment, where he was indicted of two several points. What they were I have forgotten, but as I remember one of them was for denying the oaths of allegiance...

At which words, he being suddenly interrupted by one of the preachers, who told him he held it no sin to kill the King, he utterly denied that, and did abjure all such thoughts, and held them as most wicked and abominable sins. The minister answered again, 'But if a man should determine to kill the King, the Pope would forgive him that sin.' He denied that also, and said that 'the Pope neither would or could do it, but if a man had committed a sin, after hearty repentance, contrition, and satisfaction, &c ... If a man had committed a sin and was truly repentant, the Pope both might and would forgive him ... And so for the killing of a King, if a madman killed a king, and were heartily sorry and repentant for it, God forbid that you and I should then deny that his sin might be forgiven him.' Then asking him how he thought of it, the minister answered that he must confess that if a man had committed a sin, and were truly repentant for it, he held his sin might be forgiven him. But although it were true doctrine, yet it was an ill instance, and dangerous to speak before a community: and so that argument ended.

Then he went on with his speech, that he was come hither to shed his blood for our Saviour's sake, Who shed His for his sins. In which respect he wished that every drop of blood that he should shed might be a thousand, wishing to have there St Laurence's gridiron to be broiled on, St Peter's cross to be hanged on, St Stephen's stones to be stone with, to be ript, ript, and ript again...

Then putting his hand into his pocket he took forth ten shillings, and gave it to the Sheriff, desiring him to distribute it among those men that took pains with him and went afoot with him through the dirt, which were those that guarded him halberts. Then he hurled forth by handfuls among the people to the quantity of 8 or 9 £. Then he gave to the Sheriff an handkerchief, and to the hangman an angel in gold, which, he said, he gave him, not to spare him, but to execute his office as he should do.

John Almond's Later Life

Then he kneeled down and said some prayers in Latin, which when he had done he rose up. Then he hurled from him among the people his beads, and another handkerchief, his band he gave away, and all his points he hurled, with his discipline for those to get them that would. Then the hangman pulled off his clothes, and he blessed all the people round about him. Then he took a gold ring off his finger, and gave it to the Sheriff, earnestly entreating him to give it to Mr Muskett (George Fisher) in Newgate, for that he gave to him to wear so long as he lived.

The Sheriff told him that he should hang till he was more than half dead. He answered they should rip him up alive as he was, if they pleased, and not to hang him at all, so willing he was to endure torment for so good a cause.

Then standing up after a pause, he said: 'There is a doctor of divinity in this company that holds opinion that no man can live chaste, which I deny, I myself having lived chaste, pure, and die a maid.' Then the hangman put the rope around his neck, and tied a handkerchief before his eyes. With a cheerful and merry countenance he willed him to tell him when he drew away the cart from under him, because he desired to die with the name of Jesus in his mouth. At which speech the minister which had conferred with him all the while in a scoffing manner, said to him that there was great virtue in that name for sure. For which audacious speech a gentleman standing by took him up very roundly.

Then he signed himself with the sign of the Cross, and said: 'In manus tuas Domine commendo spiritum meum. Redime me Domine Deus veritatis, Jesus, Jesus, Jesus, esto mihi Jesus.' And so died. Amen.[67]

Further details of his last few moments are recounted by Father Blount in a letter that he sent from London to Father Persons:

'His courage and resolution in dying made great impression in the harts of all that were present, yea, of Protestants themselves in so much that they spake exceeding well of him & blamed the bench for condemning him & some began to stagger in their religion already, in generall all pittyed him and without doubt he did much good in his so resolute death.

---

[67] Quoted in: Steele, *Blessed John Almond*, pp.16–19

'They would have persuaded the people if they could that he was one of those that approved the killing of kinges, because in a certayne occasion he had said, that there was no doubt, but that he that killed a king might (being after penitent, & sorry for his falt) be absolved and saved: The Mynisters of Tyborne would have inferred from hence that he affirmed it to be no synne to kill a king, because he said, that being penitent afterwards he might be saved.

'His hart being cast twice into the fire both tymes lept out and being kept the second tyme was conveyed to Father Blunt, a Father of the society, who keepeth it with reverence due to so pretious a relicke.'

Archbishop Ussher writes this fitting obituary notice, despite himself: 'On Saturday last, Lathom, alias Molyneux, one of the learnedest and insolentest of the Popish priests here (for so I might easily discern by the conference which I had with him and his fellows at Newgate, was executed at Tyburn.'[68]

According to Anstruther in *The Seminary Priests – Volume 2 Early Stuarts 1603–1659*, John Almond's bones were sent to Spain with those of Thomas Maxwell who was hanged, drawn and quartered at Tyburn on 1 July 1616:

After darkness that day a party of 20 Spanish and English Catholics retrieved the quartered body and 'carried it away in order to a more decent interment'. It was indeed put in acid at the ambassador's house and eventually smuggled to Spain together with the bones of John Almond. They were deposited in the Franciscan convent of St Simon on the Isle of Rondonela off the NW coast of Spain and near the Castle of Gondomar on the mainland. A visit from Drake underlined their insecurity and they were brought ashore and placed in the chapel of St Benito de Gondomar adjoining the castle ... Later they disappeared and were discovered with full documentation in 1912 by the descendant of the ambassador El Conde de Gondomar immured in his chapel of St Ann at Gondomar.[69]

---

[68] Ibid., pp.19–20
[69] Anstruther, *The Seminary Priests*, p.215

The World Shortly After John Almond's Martyrdom

THE PILGRIM FATHERS – 1620

A Puritan was a member of the more extreme English Protestants who were dissatisfied with the Anglican Church settlement and sought a further purification of the English Church from Roman Catholic elements. Their theology was basically that of John Calvin. At first they limited themselves to attacking 'popish' practices – church ornaments, vestments and Marprelate tracts. However, James I resisted their attempts to change Anglican dogma, ritual and organisation voiced at the Hampton Court Conference. The term 'Puritan' covers many groups and attitudes and remains an area of historical debate.

In our century, the term 'pilgrim fathers' is accepted as something hallowed and antique. Yet it is of relatively recent date. The band of pioneers who sailed for the new world most likely saw themselves as saints, in the early Christian manner. Opponents called them 'Brownist' or 'separatists' – Protestants who wished to cut themselves off from the established Church in England, following the lead given by the writings of Robert Brown, of Norwich and London, in the late sixteenth century.

Brown eventually returned to Anglicanism, and the pilgrims showed some flexibility, too. Richard Clifton – an early pastor – condemned too strict a view of separatism; John Robinson his successor, was willing to hear Anglican services.

Long after the settlement of New Plymouth in the 1620s, the voyagers were known as the Old Comers or the Forefathers. However, discovery of the recollections of one of the first governors, William Bradford, in the 1850s, gave impetus to use of the term 'pilgrim'. Some decades later the orator Daniel Webster had used the phrase 'pilgrim fathers', during a bicentennial address.

Most of the 104 souls who crossed the Atlantic were not separatists. Only one third belonged to that persuasion; the rest had been gathered in London and elsewhere as helpers and settlers sent along in part to safeguard the interests of financial bankers.

Of those pilgrims who had settled in Holland in the early 1600s only a minority were willing to join the voyage to America. Their pastor, John Robinson, also stayed behind, since it had been agreed he would go only if a majority volunteered. Once the settlement had been made, others ventured forth, though Robinson stayed in Leyden for the rest of his days.

In Boston, Lincolnshire, there is a special association with America that began in 1607. A group of Puritans seeking religious freedom planned to sail from Boston to Holland in a Dutch ship. The captain, however, informed against them and seven pilgrims were imprisoned in the guildhall, before being tried at Lincoln. In the guildhall – used as a town hall – there was a courtroom with cells below. A granite memorial at Scotia Creek, Fishtoft, Boston, now marks the place of their embarkation. There were no Bostonians among the pilgrim fathers who sailed for America on the *Mayflower* in 1620. In 1630, many of Boston's citizens, local Puritans and their vicar, John Cotton, made the crossing to America and founded the colony, which they named Boston. In Boston Parish Church, Lincolnshire, there is a 'Cotton Chapel' in memory of John Cotton. The pulpit in the main nave was erected in 1612 during the reign of James I – the year in which John Cotton came to be Vicar of Boston.

Manchester and Bolton were the twin centres of Puritanism in Lancashire. Without doubt they were encouraged and influenced in their beliefs by the strong connection between the textile merchants of south-east Lancashire and Puritan London, for Puritan merchants ensured Puritan spinners and weavers just as surely as Catholic landowners ensured Catholic peasants. Two of the fellows of the Collegiate Church in Manchester had

The World Shortly After John Almond's Martyrdom

particularly strong influences – Alexander Nowell of Middleton who became dean of St Paul's, and William Bourne, who worked all his life in the Manchester area. From about 1590 most of the clergy in south-east Lancashire dispensed with surplices (this is still the case in some churches there today e.g. St Mark's, Haydock, St Helens). The congregation received the bread and wine at the Communion service either sitting or standing and, as in London, Lancashire Puritans observed the whole of Sunday as a day of prayer and praise. In 1588, Lord Derby seized and destroyed one of the presses in Manchester that were printing the fanatical Puritan pamphlets known as the *Marprelate Tracts*.

The Forty Martyrs of England and Wales

Pope Paul VI canonised forty Catholics on 25 October 1970, before a crowd estimated at fifty thousand in the great basilica of St Peter's, Rome. These individuals were selected from among two hundred already beatified (Blessed), as Martyrs of England and Wales.

All had suffered martyrdom under the persecution of Catholics, which resulted from the following religious acts made in England:

- The Treason Act of 1352 (Edward III, stat.5, cap.2) – this is still the basic treason law of England. It defined treason as compassing or attempting the death of the king or his heirs.

- An act to retain the Queen's Majesty's subjects in due obedience (23 Eliz. I, cap.1, 1581) – this act made it high treason to reconcile or be reconciled to the Catholic Church or to induce others to be reconciled ('persuading to popery'). It covered 'seditious words against the Queen'.

- An act against Jesuits, seminary priests[70] and such other like disobedient persons (27 Eliz. I, cap.2, 1585) – this act made it high treason for a Catholic priest ordained abroad to come into or remain in the realm after 24 June 1559. It

---

[70] Seminary priests were Roman Catholic priests who were trained in English seminaries in Europe during the sixteenth and seventeenth centuries, when laws against Catholics were in operation. This term distinguishes these men from those trained during earlier periods.

The Forty Martyrs of England and Wales

made it felony for anyone to harbour or assist him. The sentence for a priest was that he should be hanged, drawn and quartered and, for a layman, that he be hanged. Sometimes secondary charges were also added.

Some of the forty had refused to take the Oath of Supremacy, others had become priests or had harboured priests. Among these were Jesuits, Benedictines, Franciscans, an Augustine friar and a Bridgettine. They were:

John Almond	**Secular clergy**[71]	**Lancashire**
Edmund Arrowsmith	Jesuit	Lancashire
Ambrose Barlow	Benedictine	Lancashire
John Boste	Secular clergy	Westmorland
Alexander Briant	Secular clergy	Somerset
Edmund Campion	Jesuit	London
Margaret Clitherow	Laywoman	Yorkshire
Philip Evans	Jesuit	Monmouth
Thomas Garnet	Jesuit	London
Edmund Gennings	Secular clergy	Staffordshire
Richard Gwyn	Layman	Montgomery
John Houghton	Carthusian	Essex
Philip Howard	Layman	London
John Jones	Franciscan	Clynnog Fawr
John Kemble	Secular clergy	Hertfordshire
Luke Kirby	Secular clergy	Yorkshire
Robert Lawrence	Carthusian	

---

[71] Secular clergy: religious ministers, such as deacons and priests, who do not belong to a religious order.

David Lewis	Jesuit	Abergavenny
Anne Line	Laywoman	Essex
John Lloyd	Secular clergy	Brecknockshire
Cuthbert Mayne	Secular clergy	Devon
Henry Morse	Jesuit	Norfork/Suffolk
Nicholas Own	Jesuit	
John Payne	Secular clergy	Northants
Polydore Plasden	Secular clergy	London
John Plessington	Secular clergy	Garstang
Richard Reynolds	Bridgettine	
John Rigby	Layman	Lancashire
John Roberts	Benedictine	Monmouthshire
Alban Roe	Benedictine	Suffolk
Ralph Sherwin	Secular clergy	Derbyshire
Robert Southwell	Jesuit	Norfolk
John Southworth	Secular clergy	Lancashire
John Stone	Augustinian	
John Wall	Franciscan	Lancashire
Henry Walpole	Jesuit	Norfolk
Margaret Ward	Laywoman	Cheshire
Augustine Webster	Carthusian	
Swithun Wells	Layman	Hampshire
Eustace White	Secular clergy	Lincolnshire

Bibliography

Anstruther, G O P, *The Seminary Priests – Volume 1*, Durham, St Edmund's College, 1968

—— *The Seminary Priests – Volume 2 Early Stuarts 1603–1659*, Great Wakering, Mayhew & McCrimmon, 1975

Bailey, F A, *Prescot Parish Church – Official Guide*, Gloucester, The British Publishing Company

Bagley, J J, *A History of Lancashire*, London, Phillimore, 1976

Barker, T C & Newbury, N F, *The Growth of St Helens – A Preliminary Survey*, St Helens, St Helens Library & Education Committee, 1940

Beer Barrett L, *Tudor England Observed – The World of John Stow*, Stroud, Sutton Publishing, 1998

Bowler, Dom Hugh, (ed.) *Recusant Rolls No. 2 1593–1594*, London, Catholic Truth Society, 1965

Carman, Philip S J, *Margaret Clitherow*, London, Catholic Truth Society, 1986

Catholic Truth Society, *The Martyrs of England & Wales 1535–1680*, London, Catholic Truth Society, 1978

Cawthrone, Nigel, *Public Executions: from Ancient Rome to the Present Day*, Arturus Foulsham, 2006

Challoner, Bishop, *Memoirs of Missionary Priests*, London, Burns Oates & Washbourne, 1924

Cheshire, Paul, *Kings & Queens (An Essential A–Z Guide)*, Starfine UK Past Times, 2002

Clark, Sir George Norman, *English History – A Survey*, Oxford University Press, 1971

Davies, Stevie, *A Century of Troubles*, Bath Press, 2001

Dovey, Zillah, *An Elizabethan Progress*, Alan Sutton, 1996

Dowsing, James, *Places of the Pilgrim Fathers – in England & the Netherlands*, Sunrise Press, 1991

Farmer, David Hugh, *The Oxford Dictionary of Saints*, Oxford University Press, 1978

Fraser, Antonia, *The Gunpowder Plot – Terror of Faith in 1605*, Mandarin, 1997

—— *King James VI of Scotland I of England*, Sphere, 1977

Golding, Claud, *They Made History – Fascinating Stories of the Extraordinary People Who Made History*, Bristol, Siena Publishing, 1998

Hart-Davies, *What the Tudors & Stuarts Did for Us*, London, Pan Macmillan, 2002

Hemingway, Vincent, *The Gunpowder Plot*, Throckmorton Estates, 1994

Hogge, Alice, *God's Secret Agents*, London, Harper Perennial, 2005

Hylson-Smith, Kenneth, *The Churches in England – Volume 1 1558–1688*

LPRS, *The Registers of Childwall – Part One 1557–1680,* Lancashire Parish Register Society

Mellor, E F, *This Our Heritage – All Saints, Childwall*, Childwall, All Saints Church, 1958

Moorman, J R H, *A History of the Church in England*, London, A&C Black, 1953

Morrile, John (ed.), *The Oxford Illustrated History of Tudor and Stuart Britain*, UK, BCA, 1996

O'Day, Rosemary, *The Longman Companion to the Tudor Age*, London, Longmans, 1995

Spufford, Margaret, *The World of Rural Dissenters 1520–1725*, Cambridge University Press, 1995

Starkey, David, *Elizabeth*, London, Vincent, 2001

Steele, Thomas, *Prescot Churchwardens' Accounts 1635–1663*, Record Society of Lancashire and Cheshire, 2002

Bibliography

Steele, William, *Blessed John Almond*, London, The Office of the Vice-Postulation, 1962

Stewart-Brown, R, *A History of the Manor and Township of Allerton in the County of Lancaster*, Brown, 1911

Stonor, Robert Julian, *Liverpool's Hidden Story*, Birchley Hall Press, 1957

Tibbles, A J, *Speke Hall*, Merseyside County Council, 1983

Tindal Hart, Arthur, *The Man in the Pew 1558–1660*, UK, Baker, 1966

Walsh, James S J, *Forty Martyrs of England and Wales*, London, Catholic Truth Society, 1997

Watkins, Susan, *Elizabeth I and Her World – In Public and Private*, Thames Hudson Ltd, 2007

Weekley, Ernest, *Romance of Names (1914)*, USA, Kessinger Publishing, 2003

Weir, Alison, *Children of England – The Heirs of King Henry VIII*, London, Jonathan Cape, 1996

Whale, Derek, *Lost Villages of Liverpool – Second Edition*, Merseyside, T Stephenson & Sons Ltd

Printed in the United Kingdom
by Lightning Source UK Ltd.
133443UK00001B/34-42/P